SOUTHERN KETO

Infusing Low-Carb Recipes With a Southern Twist

High Fat Recipes With Proven Meal Plan

PIPER CLARK

Table of Contents

PART I 12

Keto Recipes 13

Chapter 1: Gourmet Recipes 15

Creamy Garlic Chicken 15

Mediterranean Lemon Herb Chicken Salad 17

Garlic Butter Scallops and Steak 20

Fried Chicken 22

Lime Chile Steak Fajitas 24

Spaghetti Squash With Stuffed Lasagna 27

Zucchini Boats With Stuffed Tuna 29

Spinach and Goat Cheese Stuffed Breast of Chicken 31

Chapter 2: Quick and Easy Recipes 33

Antipasto Salad 33

Feta Cheese and Chicken Plate 35

Cheese Omelet 36

Baked Salmon and Pesto 37

Pork Chops and Blue Cheese Sauce 39

Green Pepper and Pork Stir-Fry 41

Broccoli With Fried Chicken 43

Fried Eggs With Pork and Kale 44

Chapter 3: Sweet Recipes 45

Sugar Cinnamon Donuts 45

Mug Brownie 47

Mini Cheesecake 49

Keto Fudge 52
Peanut Butter Hearts 53
Peanut Butter and White Chocolate Blondies 54
Low Carb Ice Cream 55
Chocolate Donut 57
Chapter 4: Savory Recipes 59
Keto McMuffin 59
Sausage Hash With Rainbow Chard 61
Veggie and Chicken Sausage Skillet 63
Cheese and Crispy Salami 64
Buffalo Chicken Sandwich 65
Cream Cheese and Salmon Bites 67
Turkey Patties 70
Chapter 5: Poultry and Meat Recipes 71
Beef Cabbage Skillet 71
Meatball Casserole 73
Beef Taquitos 75
Chicken Wings 77
Roasted Leg of Chicken 79
Chapter 6: Staple Recipes 82
Keto Waffles 82
Cookie Dough 84
Baked Tofu 85
Cauliflower Fried Rice 86
PART II 87
Vegan Cookbook 88
Chapter 1: Breakfast Recipes 91

Shamrock Sandwich 91
Breakfast Burrito 93
Gingerbread Waffles 96
Green Chickpeas And Toast 98
Asparagus And Tomato Quiche 100
Breakfast Bowl 102
Tofu Pancakes 104
Chapter 2: Side Dish Recipes 106
Baked Beans 106
Baked Potato Wedges 108
Black Beans And Quinoa 109
Roasted Lemon Garlic Broccoli 110
Spicy Tofu 111
Spanish Rice 113
Pepper And Lemon Pasta 114
Chapter 3: High Protein Recipes 115
Kale Salad With Spicy Tempeh Bits And Chickpeas 115
Protein Bars 118
Tofu And Spinach Scramble 120
Vegan Tacos 121
Grilled Tofu Steaks And Spinach Salad 123
Corn, Quinoa, And Edamame Salad 126
Lentil Soup 127
Chapter 4: Dessert Recipes 129
Chocolate Pudding 129
Orange Cake 131
Pumpkin Tofu Pie 133

Vegan Brownie....135
Vegan Cupcake....136
Vanilla Cake....138
Miracle Fudge....140
Chapter 5: Sauces & Dips Recipes....142
Tomato Jam....142
Walnut Kale Pesto....143
Ranch Dressing....144
PART III....146
Smoothie Diet Recipes....147
Chapter 1: Fruit Smoothies....148
Quick Fruit Smoothie....148
Triple Threat Smoothie....150
Tropical Smoothie....151
Fruit and Mint Smoothie....152
Banana Smoothie....154
Dragon Fruit Smoothie....156
Kefir Blueberry Smoothie....158
Ginger Fruit Smoothie....160
Fruit Batido....162
Banana Peanut Butter Smoothie....163
Chapter 2: Breakfast Smoothies....164
Berry Banana Smoothie....164
Berry Surprise....165
Coconut Matcha Smoothie....167
Cantaloupe Frenzy....168
Berry Lemon Smoothie....169

Orange Glorious 171
Grapefruit Smoothie 172
Sour Smoothie 173
Ginger Orange Smoothie 174
Cranberry Smoothie 175
Creamsicle Smoothie 177
Sunshine Smoothie 178
Chapter 3: Vegetable Smoothies 179
Mango Kale Berry Smoothie 179
Breakfast Pink Smoothie 180
Butternut Squash Smoothie 182
Zucchini and Wild Blueberry Smoothie 183
Cauliflower and Blueberry Smoothie 184
Immunity Booster Smoothie 185
Ginger, Carrot, and Turmeric Smoothie 188
Romaine Mango Smoothie 190
Fig Zucchini Smoothie 191
Carrot Peach Smoothie 192
Sweet Potato and Mango Smoothie 194
Carrot Cake Smoothie 195
Chapter 4: Green Smoothies 196
Kale Avocado Smoothie 196
Celery Pineapple Smoothie 198
Cucumber Mango and Lime Smoothie 199
Kale, Melon, and Broccoli Smoothie 201
Kiwi Spinach Smoothie 203
Avocado Smoothie 204

PART IV 205

Chapter 1: The Fundamentals of a Low Sugar Diet for Diabetics 206

Chapter 2: Benefits of a Low Sugar Diet for Diabetics 209

Chapter 3: Savory Recipe Ideas 212

Savory Idea #1: Tangy Cabbage Treat..212

Savory Idea #2: Low-carb Egg &Veggie Bites 214

Savory Idea #3: Yummy Chicken Dee-light 216

Savory Idea #4: Low-carb Fried Chicken Surprise 218

Savory Idea #5: Low-Sugar Beef Explosion 220

Savory Idea #6: Tangy Pork Extravaganza 222

Savory Idea #7: Filet & Cheese Supreme 224

Savory Idea #8: Quick and Easy Low-carb Chips 225

Savory Idea #9: Unbelievably Low-carb South Treat 226

Savory Idea #10: Low-sugar Italian Snack Option 228

Chapter 4: Gourmet Recipe Ideas 230

Gourmet Idea #1: Tasty Chicken and Veggie Pot..230

Gourmet Idea #2: Delicious Low-sugar Chicken Meal..231

Gourmet Idea #3: Italian Chicken Dinner Delight..233

Gourmet Idea #4: Yummy Lemon Beef Surprise 235

Gourmet Idea #5: Gourmet Sirloin Option 236

Gourmet Idea #6: Unbelievably Low-sugar Surprise..238

Gourmet Idea #7: Low-carb Salmon Delight 239

Gourmet Idea #8: Shrimp-Avocado Treat 241

Gourmet Idea #9: Gourmet Hot Pot Surprise..242

Gourmet Idea #10: Low-carb Tuna Wraps Treat 243

Chapter 5: Quick and Easy Recipe Ideas 244

Quick and Easy Idea #1: Quick and Easy Veggie Treat....244
Quick and Easy Idea #2: Spicy Egg and Veggie Dash....246
Quick and Easy Idea #3: Low-sugar Hot Cake Surprise....248
Quick and Easy Idea #4: Cheesy Veggie Bites....250
Quick and Easy Idea #5: Low-carb Pudding Dee-light....252
Quick and Easy Idea #6: Tangy Egg Salad....253
Quick and Easy Idea #7: Cheesy Egg Cups....255
Quick and Easy Idea #8: Asparagus Appetizer/Side Salad....257
Quick and Easy Idea #9: Low-carb Pork Treat....258
Quick and Easy Idea #10: Easy Fish Delight....259
Chapter 6: Low-Carb Recipe Ideas....260
Low-Carb Recipe Idea #1: Balsamic Roast Delight....260
Low-Carb Recipe Idea #2: Burger Calzone Treat....262
Low-Carb Recipe Idea #3: Steak Skillet Nacho....264
Low-Carb Recipe Idea #4: Portobello Burger Meal....266
Low-Carb Recipe Idea #5: Low-carb Super Chili....268
Low-Carb Recipe Idea #6: "You won't believe it's low-carb" Chicken Parmesan....269
Low-Carb Recipe Idea #7: Tangy Coconut Chicken....271
Low-Carb Recipe Idea #8: Slow cook Chicken Casserole....274
Low-Carb Recipe Idea #9: Low-carb Roll Up Treat....275
Low-Carb Recipe Idea #10: Cauliflower Cheese Surprise....276
Chapter 7: 7-day Sample Low Sugar Diet Plan....277

PART I

Keto Recipes

The keto diet is a high-fat and low-carb diet that comes with various health benefits. It has been found that this diet can help you lose weight and improve the condition of your health. It might also show some positive effects on cancer, diabetes, Alzheimer's, and epilepsy. This diet's main aim is to reduce the intake of carbs drastically and replace the same with healthy fats. When you reduce the consumption of carbs, the body will enter a metabolic state known as ketosis. During ketosis, the body will try its best to burn the body fat for generating energy. It will also be turning the liver fat into ketones that supply energy to the brain.

A keto diet is a very effective way of losing weight. The best aspect of this diet is that you can lose bodyweight without counting calories. The reason behind this is that the diet will be so filling that you will not have frequent cravings. It has been found that people who follow a keto diet can lose 2.5 times more weight when compared to those people who follow a calorie-restrictive diet. The keto diet can also deal with type 2 diabetes, metabolic, and prediabetes syndrome. Some other benefits of the keto diet are:

- **Cancer:** This diet can help suppress the growth of tumors and might also help in treating various types of cancer.
- **Heart diseases:** The keto diet can help deal with various chronic heart conditions such as heart attack, stroke, and others.

- **Polycystic ovary:**This diet is well known for reducing insulin levels that can help in dealing with polycystic ovary.

There are certain food items that you will need to include while following this diet.

- **Fatty fish**: Trout, salmon, mackerel, tuna
- **Meat**: Steak, sausage, red meat, ham, chicken, bacon, turkey
- **Seeds and nuts**: Walnuts, almonds, pumpkin seeds, flax seeds, chia seeds
- **Oils**: Coconut oil, olive oil, avocado oil

A keto diet is an excellent option for all those who have diabetes, overweight or want to improve the health of their metabolism. I have included some tasty and easy keto recipes that you can include in your diet plan.

Chapter 1: Gourmet Recipes

If you are looking for some tasty keto gourmet recipes, this section has got what you are searching for. So, let's have a look at them.

Creamy Garlic Chicken

Total Prep & Cooking Time: Twenty-five minutes

Yields: Six servings

Nutrition Facts: Calories: 348 | Protein: 28g | Carbs: 6.3g | Fat: 22.3g | Fiber: 0.9g

Ingredients

- Two pounds of chicken breasts (sliced thinly)
- Two tbsps. of olive oil
- One cup of each
    - Heavy cream
    - Spinach (chopped)
- Half cup of each
    - Chicken stock
    - Parmesan cheese
    - Sun-dried tomatoes
- One tsp. of each
    - Italian seasoning
    - Garlic powder

Method:

1. Take an iron skillet and add olive oil in it. After the oil gets hot, add the chicken and cook for five minutes. Remove the pieces of chicken from the skillet. Keep aside.

2. Add chicken stock, heavy cream, Italian seasoning, garlic powder, and parmesan cheese in the skillet. Whisk the mixture on medium flame until the sauce thickens. Add tomatoes and spinach. Simmer the mixture for two minutes until the spinach wilts.

3. Addcooked chicken into the prepared sauce. Cook for two minutes.

4. Serve hot.

Mediterranean Lemon Herb Chicken Salad

Total Prep & Cooking Time: Twenty-five minutes

Yields: Four servings

Nutrition Facts: Calories: 326 | Protein: 22.3g | Carbs: 12g | Fat: 20.1g | Fiber: 6.2g

Ingredients

- Two tbsps. of each
  - Olive oil
  - Water
  - Parsley (chopped)
  - Red wine vinegar
  - Basil (dried)
  - Garlic (minced)
- One lemon (juiced)
- One tsp. of each
  - Salt
  - Oregano
- One pound of chicken thighs

For the salad:

- Four cups of lettuce leaves (washed)
- One cucumber (diced)
- Two tomatoes (diced)
- One onion (sliced)
- One avocado (sliced)
- One-third cup of kalamata olives (sliced)
- Wedges of lemon (for serving)

Method:

1. Whisk all the marinade ingredients in a bowl. Pour half of the marinade in a shallow dish. Store the remaining marinade for the dressing.
2. Add the pieces of chicken in the marinade dish and marinate for half an hour.
3. Mix all the ingredients for the salad in a mixing bowl and keep aside.
4. Heat some oil in a grill pan. Add the marinated chicken and cook for five minutes on each side until browned on all sides.
5. Slice the chicken pieces.
6. Serve the salad with chicken from the top. Drizzle some of the marinade and serve with lemon wedges.

Garlic Butter Scallops and Steak

Total Prep & Cooking Time: Thirty minutes

Yields: Two servings

Nutrition Facts: Calories: 280 | Protein: 23.1g | Carbs: 1.2g | Fat: 1.3g | Fiber: 0.3g

Ingredients

- Two fillets of beef tenderloin
- Black pepper and kosher salt (according to taste)
- Three tbsps. of butter
- Ten sea scallops

For the sauce:

- Three garlic cloves (minced)
- Six tbsps. of butter (cubed)
- Two tbsps. of each
    - Chives (chopped)
    - Parsley (chopped)
- One tbsp. of lemon juice
- Two tsps. of lemon zest

- Black pepper and kosher salt (according to taste)

Method:

1. Take an iron skillet and heat it over medium flame for ten minutes.
2. Season the steak with pepper and salt.
3. Add two tbsps. of butter in the skillet. Add the steak and cook for six minutes on each side. Cook until the steak reaches your desired doneness.
4. Keep the steak aside and heat one tbsp. of butter in the skillet.
5. Remove the muscles from the small side of the scallops and wash them with cold running water.
6. Season the scallops with pepper and salt. Cook the scallops on each side for three minutes.
7. For making the sauce, add garlic and butter in a skillet. Stir for one minute. Add chives, lemon zest, parsley, and lemon juice. Add pepper and salt for seasoning.
8. Serve the scallops and steak with butter sauce from the top.

Fried Chicken

Total Prep & Cooking Time: Fifty minutes

Yields: Twelve servings

Nutrition Facts: Calories: 305 | Protein: 38.2g | Carbs: 0.6g | Fat: 12.3g | Fiber: 0.5g

Ingredients

- Four ounces of pork rinds
- Two tsps. of thyme (dried)
- One tsp. of each

- Black pepper
- Salt
- Oregano (dried)

- Half tsp. of garlic powder
- One-third tsp. of paprika (smoked)
- Twelve chicken legs
- One large egg
- Two ounces of mayonnaise
- Three tbsps. of Dijon mustard

Method:

1. Crush the pork rinds for making powder texture. Leave some of the big pieces.
2. Preheat the oven at 200 degrees Celsius.
3. Mix salt, pork rinds, thyme, pepper, garlic powder, oregano, and paprika. Spread out the prepared mixture on a large flat dish.
4. Combine Dijon mustard, egg, and mayonnaise in a bowl. Dip the chicken legs in the egg mixture and then roll in the mixture of pork rind. Coat well.
5. Place the legs of chicken on a baking tray. Bake for forty minutes.
6. Serve hot.

Lime Chile Steak Fajitas

Total Prep & Cooking Time: Twenty-five minutes

Yields: Four servings

Nutrition Facts: Calories: 419 | Protein: 23.1g | Carbs: 12g | Fat: 25.6g | Fiber: 5.1g

Ingredients

For the marinade:

- Two tbsps. of olive oil
- One-third cup of lime juice
- Three tbsps. of cilantro (chopped)
- Two garlic cloves (chopped)
- One tsp. of brown sugar
- Three-fourth tsp. of chili flakes
- Half tsp. of cumin (ground)
- One tsp. of salt
- One pound of steak

For the fajitas:

- Three capsicums (different colors, sliced)
- One avocado (sliced)
- One onion (sliced)

For serving:

- Tortillas
- Sour cream

Method:

1. Combine all the marinade ingredients in a bowl. Keep aside half of the marinade. Pour the remaining marinade in a flat dish and marinate the steak.
2. Heat one tsp. of oil in a skillet. Add the steak and grill for five minutes on each side. Allow the steak to cool down for five minutes.
3. Wipe the skillet and brush some oil. Fry the capsicums along with the strips of onion. Add the reserved marinade, pepper, and salt.
4. For serving the steak, slice the steak. Arrange steak, sour cream, avocado, and cooked veggies in the tortillas. Serve with marinade and cilantro from the top.

Spaghetti Squash With Stuffed Lasagna

Total Prep & Cooking Time: Two hours

Yields: Four servings

Nutrition Facts: Calories: 280 | Protein: 23.1g | Carbs: 6.7g | Fat: 21.3g | Fiber: 0.2g

Ingredients

- One pound of Italian sausage
- One spaghetti squash
- One cup of pasta sauce (low-carb)
- One-fourth cup of ricotta
- One-third cup of mozzarella
- Half cup of parmesan
- Pepper and salt (according to taste)
- Parsley (for garnishing)

Method:

1. Cut spaghetti squash in half. Remove the seeds. Bake the squash in the oven with the cut side down in one inch of water. Bake for fifty minutes at 200 degrees Celsius.

2. Take a skillet and add the sausage. Cook until browned and add pasta sauce. Simmer for ten minutes and add seasonings.
3. Take out the baked squash and scrape the inside portion with the help of a fork. Add the squash strands in a bowl.
4. Combine the strands with ricotta, meat sauce, and cheese.
5. Stuff the squash shells with the mixture and arrange in a baking sheet. Top with mozzarella.
6. Bake the squash for fifteen minutes until the cheese melts.
7. Serve with parsley from the top.

Zucchini Boats With Stuffed Tuna

Total Prep & Cooking Time: Thirty minutes

Yields: Two servings

Nutrition Facts: Calories: 412 | Protein: 37.2g | Carbs: 23.2g | Fat: 18.3g | Fiber: 10.6g

Ingredients

- Two tsps. of avocado oil
- Half red bell pepper (diced)
- Two cans of wild tuna
- Half cup of salsa
- Two zucchinis
- Pepper and salt
- Half tsp. of cumin

For salsa:

- One avocado (cubed)
- One-fourth cup of cilantro (chopped)
- Three tbsps. of onion (minced)
- Two tsps. of lime juice

Method:

1. Take a frying pan and heat oil in it. Add diced pepper and sauté for two minutes. Remove the pepper and add tuna. Cook for four minutes.
2. Add salsa to the pan. Combine well.
3. Trim the zucchini ends. Slice them in half, lengthwise. Use a spoon for scraping out the flesh. Sprinkle some cumin, pepper, and salt.
4. Fill the zucchini shells with tuna mixture.
5. Preheat your oven at 200 degrees Celsius.
6. Bake the zucchini for twenty minutes.
7. Mix the ingredients for the salsa in a large small mixing bowl.
8. Serve the zucchini boats with salsa by the side.

Spinach and Goat Cheese Stuffed Breast of Chicken

Total Prep & Cooking Time: Forty-five minutes

Yields: Four servings

Nutrition Facts: Calories: 229 | Protein: 27.8g | Carbs: 4.9g | Fat: 13.7g | Fiber: 2.8g

Ingredients

- Four breasts of chicken
- Two tbsps. of olive oil
- Four cups of spinach
- Half tsp. of garlic powder
- Two ounces of goat cheese
- One onion (sliced)
- Eight ounces of bella mushrooms
- One tsp. of thyme
- Pepper and salt (for seasoning)

Method:

1. Heat the oven at 175 degrees Celsius.

2. Use a sharp knife for cutting slits on the upper side of the chicken breasts. Drizzle the breasts with olive oil, pepper, and salt. Keep aside.

3. Take a large skillet and heat half tbsp. of oil in it. Add spinach and cook for two minutes. Add garlic powder and cook until the spinach wilts.

4. Transfer spinach to a bowl. Add the goat cheese. Combine well.

5. Stuff the slits of the chicken breasts with the cheese and spinach mixture.

6. Heat one tbsp. of oil in the same skillet. Add mushrooms, onion, and thyme. Season with pepper and salt. Cook until the onions caramelize. Move the cooked veggies to a side to make some room for the chicken breasts.

7. Add the stuffed chicken breasts to the skillet.

8. Put the skillet in the oven. Bake for thirty minutes.

9. Serve hot.

Chapter 2: Quick and Easy Recipes

When you are short of time, opting for quick and easy recipes is the best option. So, I have included some easy recipes in this section that you can make without any hassle.

Antipasto Salad

Total Prep & Cooking Time: Thirty minutes

Yields: Two servings

Nutrition Facts: Calories: 510 | Protein: 36.8g | Carbs: 12.4g | Fat: 61g | Fiber: 10.6g

Ingredients

- Ten ounces of lettuce (chopped in pieces)
- Two tbsps. of parsley (chopped)
- Five ounces of mozzarella cheese (sliced)
- Three ounces of each
    - Salami (sliced thinly)
    - Prosciutto (sliced thinly)
- Four ounces of canned artichokes (quartered)
- Two cups of roasted red pepper
- One ounce of each
    - Sun-dried tomatoes (chopped)
    - Olives (sliced)
- One-third cup of basil

- One chili pepper (chopped)
- Half tbsp. of salt
- Four tbsps. of olive oil

Method:

1. Distribute the leaves of lettuce on serving plates or on a large dish.
2. Add parsley from the top.
3. Layer all the ingredients of antipasto.
4. In a bowl, mix chopped chili, basil, and salt. Crush the ingredients using a wooden spoon.
5. Sprinkle the crushed mixture over the salad and serve with olive oil from the top.

Feta Cheese and Chicken Plate

Total Prep & Cooking Time: Ten minutes

Yields: Two servings

Nutrition Facts: Calories: 810 | Protein: 63.3g | Carbs: 8.7g | Fat: 71g | Fiber: 3.2g

Ingredients

- Five-hundred grams of rotisserie chicken
- Two cups of feta cheese
- Two tomatoes
- Three cups of lettuce
- Ten olives
- One-third cup of olive oil
- Pepper and salt (according to taste)

Method:

1. Arrange chicken, lettuce, cheese, and olives on a plate. Slice the tomatoes and arrange them on the plate.
2. Sprinkle pepper and salt for seasoning.
3. Serve with olive oil from the top.

Note: If you do not want to use rotisserie chicken, you can cook the chicken from scratch.

Cheese Omelet

Total Prep & Cooking Time: Fifteen minutes

Yields: Two servings

Nutrition Facts: Calories: 797 | Protein: 37.2g | Carbs: 3.9g | Fat: 74.2g | Fiber: 0.1g

Ingredients

- Half cup of butter
- Six large eggs
- One cup of cheddar cheese (shredded)
- Pepper and salt (according to taste)

Method:

1. Break the eggs in a bowl. Add the cheese and whisk. Season with pepper and salt.
2. Take a medium-sized pan and melt some butter in it. Add the whisked egg mixture and allow it to set for two minutes.
3. Reduce the flame and cook for four minutes on each side. Add the leftover cheese.
4. Fold the omelet in half. Cook for one more minute.
5. Serve hot.

Baked Salmon and Pesto

Total Prep & Cooking Time: Thirty minutes

Yields: Four servings

Nutrition Facts: Calories: 625 | Protein: 48.3g | Carbs: 3.2g | Fat: 89g | Fiber: 0.7g

Ingredients

- Four tbsps. of pesto
- One cup of mayonnaise
- Half cup of Greek yogurt
- Pepper and salt (according to taste)

For the salmon:

- Four fillets of salmon
- Four tbsps. of green pesto
- Pepper and salt (for seasoning)

Method:

1. Grease a baking dish with some oil. Place the fillets of salmon on the dish with the skin-side down. Spread green pesto on the fillets and season with pepper and salt.
2. Bake the salmon for thirty minutes at 200 degrees Celsius.
3. Stir the ingredients for the sauce in a bowl.
4. Serve the salmon with sauce from the top.

Pork Chops and Blue Cheese Sauce

Total Prep & Cooking Time: Twenty minutes

Yields: Four servings

Nutrition Facts: Calories: 669 | Protein: 53.2g | Carbs: 4.3g | Fat: 60.1g | Fiber: 1.6g

Ingredients

- Two cups of blue cheese
- One cup of whipping cream (heavy)
- Four pork chops
- Seven ounces of green beans
- Two tbsps. of butter
- Pepper and salt

Method:

1. Crumble the blue cheese in a pot. Place the pot over medium flame and allow the cheese to melt.
2. Add whipping cream in the melted cheese and mix well. Simmer for two minutes.
3. Season the chops using pepper and salt.
4. Take an iron skillet and heat some oil in it. Add the chops and cook for four minutes on each side.
5. Add the juices from the pan in the sauce and stir.
6. Trim the beans. Heat some oil butter in the skillet and sauté the beans for two minutes.
7. Serve the pork chops with cheese sauce from the top and beans by the side.

Green Pepper and Pork Stir-Fry

Total Prep & Cooking Time: Twenty-five minutes

Yields: Two servings

Nutrition Facts: Calories: 678 | Protein: 31.2g | Carbs: 5.3g | Fat: 71.3g | Fiber: 4.6g

Ingredients

- Four ounces of butter
- Four-hundred grams of pork shoulder (cut in strips)
- Two bell pepper (green, sliced)
- Two scallions (sliced)
- Half cup of almond
- One tsp. of chili paste
- Pepper and salt

Method:

1. Heat butter in a wok. Add the meat strips in the butter and cook for five minutes until browned.
2. Add the chili paste along with veggies. Cook for two minutes. Add pepper and salt.
3. Serve the stir-fry with almonds from the top.

Broccoli With Fried Chicken

Total Prep & Cooking Time: Thirty minutes

Yields: Two servings

Nutrition Facts: Calories: 633 | Protein: 30.1g | Carbs: 5.3g | Fat: 64.3g | Fiber: 3.6g

Ingredients

- Nine ounces of broccoli
- One cup of butter
- Ten ounces of chicken thighs (boneless)
- Pepper and salt
- Half cup of mayonnaise

Method:

1. Rinse the broccoli thoroughly under running water. Trim the florets along with the stem.
2. Heat some butter in a pan.
3. Season the chicken thighs. Add the chicken to the pan and cook them for five minutes on all sides.
4. Add some more butter in the pan and add the broccoli. Toss the broccoli and chicken and cook for two minutes.
5. Serve with mayonnaise from the top.

Fried Eggs With Pork and Kale

Total Prep & Cooking Time: Twenty-five minutes

Yields: Three servings

Nutrition Facts: Calories: 910 | Protein: 24g | Carbs: 7.6g | Fat: 89g | Fiber: 6.3g

Ingredients

- One cup of kale
- Three ounces of butter
- Six ounces of bacon or pork belly (smoked)
- One ounce of walnuts
- Four large eggs
- Pepper and salt

Method:

1. Chop the kale and wash them under cold water.
2. Melt some butter in a skillet and cook the kale for two minutes until the edges are slightly browned.
3. Remove kale from the skillet and keep aside. Add bacon or pork belly in the same skillet and sear until crispy.
4. Add the kale in the skillet along with walnuts. Toss the ingredients.
5. Heat butter in another pan and fry the eggs sunny side up. Add pepper and salt for seasoning.
6. Serve the eggs with kale mixture by the side.

Chapter 3: Sweet Recipes

Even when you are on a diet, you don't have to compromise on satisfying your sweet tooth. So, I have included some easy to make sweet keto recipes in this section.

Sugar Cinnamon Donuts

Total Prep & Cooking Time: Twenty-five minutes

Yields: Twelve servings

Nutrition Facts: Calories: 82 | Protein: 2.3g | Carbs: 1.9g | Fat: 7.8g | Fiber: 0.3g

Ingredients

- Two eggs
- One-fourth cup of almond milk
- One-fourth tsp. of apple cider vinegar

- One tsp. of vanilla extract
- Two tbsps. of butter
- One-third cup of sweetener
- One cup of fine almond flour
- Half tbsp. of coconut flour
- One tsp. of cinnamon (ground)
- One and a half tsp. of baking powder
- Half tsp. of baking soda
- Half cup of salt

For sugar cinnamon coating:

- One-fourth cup of granulated erythritol
- One tsp. of cinnamon (ground)
- Two tbsps. of butter

Method:

1. Whisk together almond milk, eggs, butter, vinegar, vanilla extract, and sweetener. Combine until smooth.

2. Combine coconut flour, almond flour, baking powder, cinnamon, salt, and baking soda in a bowl. Add all the dry ingredients slowly to the mixture of wet ingredients. Stir well until combined.

3. Transfer the donut batter into a donut pan.

4. Bake the donuts for fifteen minutes at 175 degrees Celsius.

5. Take out the donuts and keep aside for cooling.

6. Stir together cinnamon and sweetener in a bowl.

7. Melt the butter in a pan.

8. Take the donuts and dunk them in the butter. Roll the donuts in the cinnamon coating.

Mug Brownie

Total Prep & Cooking Time: Ten minutes

Yields: Two servings

Nutrition Facts: Calories: 194 | Protein: 7.9g | Carbs: 7.6g | Fat: 16.5g | Fiber: 6.7g

Ingredients

- Two tbsps. of almond flour
- One tbsp. of each
    - Granulated sweetener
    - Cocoa powder
    - Almond butter
    - Chocolate chips
- One-eighth tsp. of baking powder
- Three tbsps. of milk

Method:

1. Use a cooking spray for greasing cereal bowls or mugs.
2. Combine the listed dry ingredients. Mix properly.
3. Mix milk and almond butter in a separate bowl and mix well.
4. Combine the dry and wet ingredients. Mix well. Add the chocolate chips and fold well.
5. Pour the batter in the cereal bowls. Bake for six minutes.
6. Enjoy your brownie from the bowl.

Mini Cheesecake

Total Prep & Cooking Time: Three hours and twenty minutes

Yields: Six servings

Nutrition Facts: Calories: 230 | Protein: 4.7g | Carbs: 5.1g | Fat: 19.6g | Fiber: 1.8g

Ingredients

For the crust:

- Half cup of almond flour
- Two tbsps. of sweetener
- Half tsp. of cinnamon
- Two tbsps. of butter (melted)

For the filling:

- Six ounces of cream cheese (softened)
- Five tbsps. of sweetener
- One-fourth cup of sour cream
- Half tsp. of vanilla extract
- One egg
- Two tsps. of cinnamon (ground)

For the frosting:

- One tbsp. of butter (softened)
- Three tbsps. of confectioners sweetener
- One-fourth tsp. of vanilla extract
- Two tsps. of heavy cream

Method:

1. Heat the oven at 175 degrees Celsius. Line a small muffin pan with six silicone liners.
2. Whisk almond flour, cinnamon, and sweetener in a bowl. Add melted butter and mix well.
3. Divide the prepared crust among the muffin cups. Press the crust to the bottom. Bake in the oven for five minutes.
4. Beat three tbsps. of sweetener along with the cream cheese in a bowl. Add vanilla, egg, and sour cream. Beat well.
5. Reduce oven temperature to 160 degrees Celsius.
6. Whisk cinnamon and butter in a bowl.
7. Add three-fourth tbsp. of cheese mixture into the muffin cups. Sprinkle cinnamon mixture from the top.
8. Bake the muffins for fifteen minutes. Refrigerate the muffins for two hours.
9. Beat powdered sweetener and butter in a bowl. Add heavy cream and vanilla extract. Mix well.
10. Transfer the frosting to a zip-lock bag and cut a small hole at the corner.
11. Add frosting over the cheesecakes.

Keto Fudge

Total Prep & Cooking Time: One hour

Yields: Twelve servings

Nutrition Facts: Calories: 158 | Protein: 0.1g | Carbs: 0.6g | Fat: 17.9g | Fiber: 0.7g

Ingredients

- One cup of coconut oil
- One-fourth cup of each
  - Cocoa powder
  - Erythritol (powdered)
- One tsp. of vanilla extract
- One-eighth tsp. of sea salt
- Sea salt

Method:

1. Use parchment paper for lining a glass baking dish.
2. Beat sweetener and coconut oil using a hand blender. Make sure the mixture is fluffy.
3. Add vanilla extract, cocoa powder, and salt. Combine well.
4. Pour the fudge mixture in the lined dish. Smoothen the top using a spoon or spatula.
5. Refrigerate the fudge for forty minutes until it solidifies.
6. Use a sharp knife to run along the edges of the dish for taking out the fudge.
7. Cut in small cubes and serve.

Peanut Butter Hearts

Total Prep & Cooking Time: Thirty minutes

Yields: Twenty servings

Nutrition Facts: Calories: 91 | Protein: 5.1g | Carbs: 7.1g | Fat: 6.7g | Fiber: 5.2g

Ingredients

- Two cups of peanut butter
- Three-fourth cup of any sticky sweetener
- One cup of coconut flour
- One and a half cup of chocolate chips

Method:

1. Use parchment paper for lining a large glass tray.
2. Combine sticky sweetener with peanut butter on the stovetop. Combine the mixture until it melts completely.
3. Add the coconut flour and combine. In case the batter is very thin, you can add more flour.
4. Make twenty balls from the dough. Use a heart-shaped cookie cutter for pressing the dough balls for making heart shape.
5. Arrange the hearts on the lined glass tray and refrigerate.
6. Melt the chocolate chips and dip the hearts in the melted chocolate.
7. Refrigerate again for twenty minutes until firm.

Peanut Butter and White Chocolate Blondies

Total Prep & Cooking Time: Three hours and thirty-five minutes

Yields: Sixteen servings

Nutrition Facts: Calories: 102 | Protein: 3.2g | Carbs: 2.2g | Fat: 9.3g | Fiber: 1.9g

Ingredients

- Half cup of each
    - Peanut butter
    - Sweetener of your choice
- Four tbsps. of butter (softened)
- Two large eggs
- One tsp. of vanilla extract
- Three tbsps. of cocoa butter (melted)
- One-fourth cup of almond flour
- One tbsp. of coconut flour
- One cup of cocoa butter (chopped)

Method:

1. Heat the oven at 175 degrees Celsius. Use a cooking spray for greasing a baking dish.
2. Combine all the ingredients in a large bowl using a hand mixer.
3. Pour the mixture in the greased dish.
4. Bake for thirty minutes.
5. Cool the blondies and refrigerate for about three hours.
6. Cut the blondies in squares and serve.

Low Carb Ice Cream

Total Prep & Cooking Time: Five hours and thirty-five minutes

Yields: Eight servings

Nutrition Facts: Calories: 337 | Protein: 2.2g | Carbs: 3.1g | Fat: 34g | Fiber: 0.3g

Ingredients

- Three tbsps. of butter
- Three cups of heavy cream
- One-third cup of powdered allulose
- One-fourth cup of coconut oil
- One tsp. of vanilla extract
- One medium-sized bean of vanilla

Method:

1. Take a pan and heat it over medium flame. Melt butter in it. Add a two-third cup of the heavy cream along with sweetener. Boil the mixture and simmer for thirty minutes.
2. Pour the mixture in a bowl and let it cool at room temperature. Add vanilla seeds from the bean along with the vanilla extract. Add coconut oil and mix well.
3. Add the remaining cream and combine until smooth.
4. Pour the mixture in a container and use a spatula for smoothening the top.
5. Freeze the ice cream for five hours. Ensure that you stir the ice cream mixture after every thirty minutes for the first two hours and then after every sixty minutes.

Chocolate Donut

Total Prep & Cooking Time: One hour and twenty-five minutes

Yields: Ten servings

Nutrition Facts: Calories: 219 | Protein: 5.1g | Carbs: 7.6g | Fat: 18.6g | Fiber: 3.1g

Ingredients

- Four eggs
- Half cup of butter (melted)
- Three tbsps. of milk
- One tsp. of stevia
- One-fourth cup of each
    - Coconut flour
    - Cocoa powder (unsweetened)
    - Sea salt
    - Baking soda

For the glaze:

- One tbsp. of avocado oil
- Three-fourth cup of chocolate chips

Method:

1. Heat the oven at 175 degrees Celsius.

2. Use a cooking spray for greasing donut pan of ten cavities.

3. Mix melted butter, eggs, and stevia, and milk in a bowl.

4. Add cocoa powder, coconut flour, baking soda, and salt.

5. Pour the mixture in the donut pan. Bake the donuts for fifteen minutes until set.

6. Let the donuts cool for fifteen minutes.

7. Add the chocolate chips in a bowl and melt in the microwave. Add avocado oil and stir.

8. Take out the donuts and dip them in the chocolate glaze.

9. Let the donuts sit for thirty minutes.

Chapter 4: Savory Recipes

In this section, I have included some tasty savory keto recipes that you can enjoy at any time of the day. So, let's have a look at them.

Keto McMuffin

Total Prep & Cooking Time: Twenty minutes

Yields: Two servings

Nutrition Facts: Calories: 610 | Protein: 24g | Carbs: 3.2g | Fat: 51.8g | Fiber: 6.9g

Ingredients

- One-fourth cup of each
  - Almond flour
  - Flaxmeal
- One-fourth tsp. of baking soda
- One egg
- Two tbsps. of heavy whipping cream
- One cup of cheddar cheese (shredded)
- Three tbsps. of water
- Salt (for seasoning)

For the filling:

- Two large eggs
- One tbsp. of butter
- Two cheddar cheese slices
- One tsp. of Dijon mustard
- Pepper and salt (for seasoning)

Method:

1. Combine all the dry ingredients. Mix well.
2. Add cream, water, and egg. Combine well using a fork.
3. Add the shredded cheese and mix.
4. Pour the mixture in greased ramekins. Microwave the mixture at high settings for two minutes.
5. Take a pan and fry the eggs. Add pepper and salt for seasoning.
6. Cut the prepared muffins in half. Spread butter on the inside portion of the muffin halves.
7. Top the muffin slices with egg, cheese, and mustard.
8. Serve immediately.

Sausage Hash With Rainbow Chard

Total Prep & Cooking Time: Twenty-five minutes

Yields: Two servings

Nutrition Facts: Calories: 570 | Protein: 25g | Carbs: 7.6g | Fat: 44.6g | Fiber: 5.6g

Ingredients

- Two-hundred grams of Swiss chard
- Two cups of cauliflower rice
- One-hundred and fifty grams of sausage meat
- Three tbsps. of lard
- Two garlic cloves (chopped)
- One tbsp. of lemon juice
- One tsp. of Dijon mustard
- Pepper and salt
- Four poached eggs

Method:

1. Chop the chard stalks into small pieces.

2. Take a greased skillet and add the sausage meat. Cook for five minutes until browned. Keep aside
3. Add the remaining lard to the same skillet. Add the garlic. Cook for one minute and add the cauliflower rice. Cook the mixture for five minutes.
4. Add the chard and Dijon mustard. Combine well. Add lemon juice and cook the mixture for two minutes. Add pepper and salt for seasoning.
5. Add the sausage meat and mix.
6. Serve with poached eggs.

Veggie and Chicken Sausage Skillet

Total Prep & Cooking Time: Thirty minutes

Yields: Four servings

Nutrition Facts: Calories: 310 | Protein: 21g | Carbs: 9.3g | Fat: 22.3g | Fiber: 2.4g

Ingredients

- Three tbsps. of butter
- Five links of chicken sausage (sliced)
- Two garlic cloves (minced)
- One red onion (cut in chunks)
- One zucchini (sliced in rounds)
- One summer squash (sliced in rounds)
- One red capsicum (cut in chunks)
- One yellow capsicum (cut in chunks)
- Six cremini mushrooms (quartered)
- Half tsp. of each
    - Red pepper flakes (crushed)
    - Italian seasoning
- Pepper and salt

Method:

1. Take an iron skillet and melt some butter in it.
2. Add the sausage, onion, and garlic. Sauté the mixture for ten minutes.
3. Add the veggies and mix well. Add pepper flakes, Italian seasoning, pepper, and salt.
4. Sauté the mixture for fifteen minutes and serve hot.

Cheese and Crispy Salami

Total Prep & Cooking Time: Twenty-five minutes

Yields: Ten servings

Nutrition Facts: Calories: 37 | Protein: 2.3g | Carbs: 1.3g | Fat: 2.7g | Fiber: 6.3g

Ingredients

- Two ounces of dried salami
- One ounce of cream cheese
- Half cup of parsley (chopped)

Method:

1. Heat the oven at 170 degrees Celsius.
2. Slice the salami into thirty slices of a quarter inch.
3. Arrange the salami on a baking pan.
4. Bake them for fifteen minutes.
5. Top the salami with cream cheese along with parsley.

Buffalo Chicken Sandwich

Total Prep & Cooking Time: Twenty-five minutes

Yields: Four servings

Nutrition Facts: Calories: 480 | Protein: 27g | Carbs: 5.1g | Fat: 30g | Fiber: 2.2g

Ingredients

- Two cups of cooked chicken (shredded)
- One-third cup of red pepper sauce
- Three tbsps. of butter
- One-fourth tsp. of each
    - Celery seed spice
    - Sea salt
    - Garlic powder
- Two tbsps. of each
    - Blue cheese crumbles
    - Celery (minced)
- Four tbsps. of ranch dressing
- Three tbsps. of mayonnaise
- Four sandwich buns

Method:

1. Take a medium saucepan and melt butter in it. Add celery seed spice, red pepper sauce, sea salt, and garlic powder. Stir well.
2. Add the chicken along with celery to the pan. Mix well and cook for two minutes.
3. Add the mayonnaise and combine.
4. Cut the buns in half. Add half cup of prepared chicken mixture on the buns. Top the chicken with one tbsp. of ranch dressing and half tbsp. of cheese crumbles.
5. Place the other halves on top and serve.

Cream Cheese and Salmon Bites

Total Prep & Cooking Time: Twenty minutes

Yields: Ten servings

Nutrition Facts: Calories: 43 | Protein: 1.3g | Carbs: 0.3g | Fat: 4.6g | Fiber: 0.6g

Ingredients

- Two eggs
- Half cup of cream
- One tbsp. of salt
- One cup of cheese (shredded)
- One-third tsp. of dill (dried)
- One-third cup of cream cheese (diced)
- Two cups of salmon (smoked, chopped)

Method:

1. Combine cream, eggs, and salt in a bowl.
2. Add cheese, cream cheese, and dill. Mix well.
3. Grease a muffin tray with butter.
4. Pour the mixture in the muffin tray. Add some pieces of salmon into each muffin.
5. Bake the mixture in the oven for twenty minutes at 180 degrees Celsius.
6. Remove the bites and serve warm.Vegetable Turkey Pesto Bolognese

Total Prep & Cooking Time: Thirty minutes

Yields: Four servings

Nutrition Facts: Calories: 270 | Protein: 20.1g | Carbs: 4.3g | Fat: 13.2g | Fiber: 1.6g

Ingredients

- Two tsps. of oil
- One pound of turkey (ground)
- One cup of onion (diced)
- Two cups of each
    - Mushrooms (sliced)
    - Zucchini (sliced)
- Three tbsps. of pesto sauce
- Pasta of your choice (cooked)
- Grated cheese

Method:

1. Take a large skillet and add some oil. Add the turkey and cook until browned. Keep aside.
2. Add onions in the same and cook for two minutes. Add mushrooms and zucchini. Mix well.
3. Add the cooked turkey and combine it. Add pesto sauce simmer for five minutes.
4. Add cooked pasta along with cheese. Stir to combine. Simmer for two minutes.
5. Serve hot.

Turkey Patties

Total Prep & Cooking Time: Thirty minutes

Yields: Four servings

Nutrition Facts: Calories: 435 | Protein: 24g | Carbs: 4.5g | Fat: 37.2g | Fiber: 2.5g

Ingredients

- Five-hundred grams of ground turkey
- Half cup of almond flour
- One hot chili pepper (finely chopped)
- Two tsps. of Dijon mustard
- Two tbsps. of each
    - Parsley (chopped)
    - Lemon juice
    - Basil (chopped)
- Half tsp. of sea salt
- One tsp. black pepper (ground)
- Two spring onions (sliced finely)
- Two tbsps. of lard
- One egg
- Two garlic cloves (crushed)

Method:

1. Combine turkey, eggs, almond flour, garlic, pepper, lemon juice, Dijon mustard, basil, parsley, black pepper, and salt. Add the spring onions and mix well.

2. Make small patties using your hands.

3. Heat lard in a pan and add the patties. Cook the patties for five minutes on each side.

4. Let the patties sit for two minutes. Serve warm with spring onions.

Chapter 5: Poultry and Meat Recipes

Meat and poultry are rich in protein and various other nutrients that you need for perfect health. In this section, you will find some tasty poultry and meat keto recipes that you can make at home.

Beef Cabbage Skillet

Total Prep & Cooking Time: Thirty minutes

Yields: Four servings

Nutrition Facts: Calories: 357 | Protein: 13g | Carbs: 27g | Fat: 7.2g | Fiber: 11.3g

Ingredients

- Half green cabbage (shredded)
- Two tbsps. of butter
- One pound of beef (ground)
- Three tbsps. of taco seasoning
- One tsp. of minced onion (dried)
- One and a half cup of Mexican cheese blend
- Pepper and salt (according to taste)

Method:

1. Take a large skillet and heat one tbsp. of butter in it. Add shredded cabbage and sauté for two minutes. Keep aside.

2. Add one tbsp. of butter in the same skillet. Add the beef. Add onion, taco seasoning, and mix well. Cook for five minutes. Add one-fourth cup of water. Add the cooked cabbage along with pepper and salt. Combine half a cup of cheese.

3. Top with leftover cheese and place the skillet in the oven. Bake for ten minutes or until the cheese melts.

Meatball Casserole

Total Prep & Cooking Time: Three hours and thirty minutes

Yields: Six servings

Nutrition Facts: Calories: 470 | Protein: 37g | Carbs: 5.4g | Fat: 33.2g | Fiber: 4.7g

Ingredients

- Two pounds of beef (ground)
- Half cup of each
    - Mozzarella cheese
    - Parmesan cheese
- Two tbsps. of coconut flour
- Two large eggs
- Three-fourth tsp. of each
    - Onion (minced)
    - Salt
- One-fourth tsp. of Italian seasoning
- Half tsp. of garlic powder
- Twenty ounce can of spaghetti sauce
- Two cups of mozzarella cheese
- One tsp. of dried basil

Method:

1. Mix the ingredients in a bowl except for the spaghetti sauce, basil, and two cups of mozzarella cheese.
2. Heat a skillet on medium flame. Add one-fourth inch of coconut oil in the skillet.
3. Scoop meatballs from the mixture and add them to the skillet.
4. Cook the meatballs for five minutes until browned.
5. Place the meatballs in the base of a crockpot.
6. Add spaghetti sauce from the top.
7. Cook the meatballs on high for three hours.
8. Take out the meatballs in a baking dish.
9. Sprinkle cheese from the top.
10. Broil the meatballs for three minutes until cheese melts.

Beef Taquitos

Total Prep & Cooking Time: Forty minutes

Yields: Six servings

Nutrition Facts: Calories: 229 | Protein: 15.7g | Carbs: 1.6g | Fat: 16.3g | Fiber: 0.3g

Ingredients

- One cup of each
  - Cheddar cheese (shredded)
  - Mozzarella cheese (shredded)
- Half cup of parmesan cheese (grated)
- Half pound of beef (ground)
- One-fourth cup of onion (minced)
- Half tsp. of each
  - Paprika
  - Chili powder
  - Salt
  - Onion powder
  - Garlic powder
- One tsp. of cumin
- One-fourth tsp. of pepper
- One-third cup of water

Method:

1. Mix chili powder, cumin, garlic powder, onion powder, pepper, salt in a cup, and some water.
2. Take a skillet and brown the beef along with the onion. Add the mixture over the beef and simmer for ten minutes.
3. Mix all the cheese in a bowl. Divide the mixture of cheese for making six balls. Use parchment paper to line a baking sheet. Place them on the sheet and bake for eight minutes.
4. Let the cheese sheets cool down for two minutes.
5. Take one spoon of the beef mixture and place it on the edge of the cheese sheets. Repeat for the remaining sheets.
6. Roll them tightly for making cigar shape.
7. Serve warm.

Chicken Wings

Total Prep & Cooking Time: Fifty minutes

Yields: Four servings

Nutrition Facts: Calories: 287 | Protein: 2.3g | Carbs: 12g | Fat: 16.3g | Fiber: 1.9g

Ingredients

- Two pounds of chicken wings
- Two tsps. of salt
- Three-fourth cup of coconut aminos
- One-fourth tsp. of each

- Onion powder
- Ginger (ground)
- Garlic powder
- Chili flakes

Method:

1. Place the wings on a baking tray.

2. Sprinkle some salt evenly on the wings.

3. Bake the chicken wings in the oven for forty minutes at 180 degrees Celsius.

4. Take a skillet and add coconut aminos. Add garlic powder, ginger, onion powder, and chili flakes. Simmer the sauce and stir until the sauce thickens.

5. Place the cooked wings in a large bowl and pour the sauce over the wings. Toss the cooked wings in the prepared sauce. Coat evenly.

6. Serve hot.

Roasted Leg of Chicken

Total Prep & Cooking Time: One hour and ten minutes

Yields: Four servings

Nutrition Facts: Calories: 687 | Protein: 27.9g | Carbs: 10.1g | Fat: 58.9g | Fiber: 6g

Ingredients

- Four legs of chicken
- Four tbsps. of olive oil
- Two tbsps. of Italian seasoning
- Pepper and salt
- Twenty ounces of each
    - Cherry tomatoes
    - Broccoli

For the garlic butter:

- Four ounces of butter
- Two cloves of garlic (smashed)
- Pepper and salt

Method:

1. Toss the legs of the chicken with seasoning and oil.
2. Place the chicken legs in a baking sheet along with the tomatoes. Bake for forty-five minutes at 150 degrees Celsius.
3. As the chicken is cooking, cut the broccoli. Divide the florets and also slice the stem. Boil them in water for five minutes, along with some salt. Drain the broccoli water.
4. For making the garlic butter, combine all the ingredients in a small bowl.
5. Serve the cooked chicken legs with tomatoes, broccoli, and garlic butter by the side.

Note: Place the chicken legs in the oven with the skin side up.

Chapter 6: Staple Recipes

In this section, I have included some simple keto recipes made from everyday staples. Let's have a look at them.

Keto Waffles

Keto Waffles

Total Prep & Cooking Time: Ten minutes

Yields: Two servings

Nutrition Facts: Calories: 160 | Protein: 21.3g | Carbs: 12.6g | Fat: 5.6g | Fiber: 10.3g

Ingredients

- Four tbsps. of coconut flour
- One tbsp. of each
    - Granulated sweetener
    - Apple sauce (unsweetened)
- One-fourth tsp. of each
    - Baking powder
    - Cinnamon
- Two-third cup of egg whites
- One-fourth cup of milk
- Half tsp. of vanilla extract
- One tsp. of coconut oil

Method:

1. Take a mixing bowl and mix the dry ingredients. Keep aside.
2. Add egg whites, vanilla extract, milk, and apple sauce in a bowl. Pour this mixture into the mixture of dry ingredients. Mix well.
3. Heat a waffle iron and grease with cooking spray or oil.
4. Add the waffle batter and cook for five minutes until fluffy and crisp.

Cookie Dough

Total Prep & Cooking Time: Ten minutes

Yields: Four servings

Nutrition Facts: Calories: 130 | Protein: 4.6g | Carbs: 4.3g | Fat: 12g | Fiber: 2.9g

Ingredients

- Half cup of almond flour
- Two tbsps. of each
  - Sticky sweetener
  - Granulated sweetener
  - Coconut flour
- One and a half tbsp. of coconut oil
- One tbsp. of chocolate chips

Method:

1. Combine coconut flour, almond flour, and granulated sugar in a bowl.
2. Add coconut oil and sticky sweetener. Mix well. Add the chocolate chips.
3. You can either enjoy the dough immediately or refrigerate it for thirty minutes.

Baked Tofu

Total Prep & Cooking Time: One hour and ten minutes

Yields: Two servings

Nutrition Facts: Calories: 131.3 | Protein: 11.3g | Carbs: 3.1g | Fat: 8.6g | Fiber: 1.7g

Ingredients

- One block of tofu (firm)
- One tbsp. of each
  - Soy sauce
  - Sesame oil
  - Tamari
- Half tsp. of each
  - Ginger
  - Garlic powder
  - Cayenne powder

Method:

1. Mix all the listed ingredients except for the tofu. Let the marinade sit for five minutes.

2. Chop the block of tofu into small pieces. Add the tofu cubes in the marinade. Refrigerate for half an hour.

3. Use parchment paper for lining a baking tray. Add the marinated tofu and bake for thirty minutes. Flip the tofu cubes halfway.

4. Serve immediately.

Cauliflower Fried Rice

Total Prep & Cooking Time: Twenty minutes

Yields: Four servings

Nutrition Facts: Calories: 135 | Protein: 7.9g | Carbs: 10.3g | Fat: 7.6g | Fiber: 8.6g

Ingredients

- Two tbsps. of sesame oil
- Two garlic cloves (finely chopped)
- One onion (finely chopped)
- Two scallions
- One-fourth cup of carrots (finely chopped)
- Eight cups of cauliflower rice
- Half cup of soy sauce
- One-fourth tsp. of cayenne pepper

Method:

1. Take a large wok and heat it over a medium flame. Addsome oil in it. Add garlic and onion. Cook for two minutes. Add scallions and carrots. Sauté for two minutes.

2. Add the cauliflower rice and combine well. Add cayenne and soy sauce. Fry for four minutes.

3. Serve the fried rice with scallions from the top.

PART II

Vegan Cookbook

The vegan diet has gained immense popularity in the past few years. With an increasing number of participants, people have made up their mind to opt for the vegan options for health, environmental, or ethical reasons. When done in the perfect way, a vegan diet can help in showcasing a wide array of health benefits, for example, better control over blood sugar and a slimmer waistline. However, when a diet is based entirely on plant derivatives, it can result in a nutrient deficiency in various cases.

Veganism is being defined as a simple way of living that aims at excluding all major forms of animal cruelty and exploitation, whether for daily food, clothing, or some other purpose. For all these reasons, this diet does not include any form of animal products, such as eggs, dairy, and meat. It has been found that all those people who tend to practice veganism are thinner and also comes with a lower BMI or body mass index when compared with non-vegans. This can easily explain the primary reason why the majority of the people are turning to this form of diet as the only way for losing extra weight.

Adopting a vegan diet can help keep the blood sugar level under proper check and type 2 diabetes. According to some studies, vegans tend to benefit from the lower levels of blood sugar, higher sensitivity to insulin, and about 77% lower risk of developing diabetes than the non-vegans. The majority of the advantages can be easily explained by the increased consumption of fiber, which can blunt the blood sugar response. Several observational studies reported that vegans could have a 74% lower risk of having increased blood pressure along with a 43% lower risk of suffering from any chronic heart disease.

There is a specific food group that you will need to omit for following a vegan diet. This group of foods includes:

- **Poultry and meat:** Lamb, beef, veal, pork, organ meat, chicken, wild meat, goose, turkey, duck, etc.
- **Dairy:** Yogurt, butter, milk, cheese, ice cream, cream, etc.

- **Seafood and fish:** Fish of all types, squid, anchovies, calamari, shrimp, lobster, mussels, crab, etc.

- **Eggs:** From ostrich, chicken, fish, quail, etc.

- **Products from bees:** Bee pollen, honey, royal jelly, etc.

- **Ingredients based on animals:** Casein, whey, egg white albumen, shellac, lactose, gelatin, L-cysteine, isinglass, omega-3 fatty acids derived from fish, vitamin D3 derived from animals, and carmine.

You can opt for alternatives such as legumes, seitan, tofu, seeds, nut butter, nuts, veggies, fruits, whole grains, etc. The cooking style will remain the same, and the only difference will be the ingredients you are going to use.

Chapter 1: Breakfast Recipes

Breakfast is an essential meal of the day that needs to be fulfilled properly. Here are some vegan breakfast recipes for you.

Shamrock Sandwich

Total Prep & Cooking Time: Fifteen minutes

Yields: One serving

Nutrition Facts: Calories: 562 | Protein: 23g | Carbs: 43.2g | Fat: 31g | Fiber: 8.3g

Ingredients:

- One sausage patty (vegan)
- One cup of kale
- Two tsps. of olive oil (extra virgin)
- One tbsp. of pepitas
- Pepper and salt (according to taste)

For the sauce:

- One tbsp. of vegan mayonnaise
- One tsp. of jalapeno (chopped)
- One-fourth tsp. of paprika (smoky)

Other ingredients:

- One-fourth of an avocado (sliced)
- One toasted English muffin

Method:

1. Start by toasting the English muffin and keep it aside.
2. Take a sauté pan and drizzle some oil in it. Add the sausage patty and cook for two minutes on each side.
3. Add pepitas and kale to the hot pan. Add pepper and salt for adjusting the taste. When the kale gets soft, and the patty gets browned, remove the pan from heat.
4. Combine the spicy sauce.
5. Assemble the sandwich with sauce on the muffins and add the patty, avocado, pepitas, and kale.

Breakfast Burrito

Total Prep & Cooking Time: Thirty minutes

Yields: Two servings

Nutrition Facts: Calories: 618 | Protein: 20.3g | Carbs: 113g | Fat: 13.7g | Fiber: 21g

Ingredients:

- Three-fourth cup of rice (rinsed)
- Two cups of water
- One-fourth tsp. of salt
- One tbsp. of lime juice
- Half cup of cilantro (chopped)

For onions and hash browns:

- Half red onion
- Four red potatoes
- Two tbsp. of olive oil
- One-fourth tsp. of each
    - Black pepper (ground)
    - Salt

For black beans:

- One cup of black beans (cooked)
- One-fourth tsp. of each
  - Chili powder
  - Cumin powder
  - Garlic powder

For the avocado slaw:

- One avocado
- Two tbsps. of lime juice
- One cup of green cabbage (sliced thinly)
- One jalapeno (sliced)
- Half tsp. of each
  - Black pepper
  - Salt

For serving:

- Two flour tortillas
- Half avocado (ripe, sliced)
- One-fourth cup of salsa

Method:

1. Boil water, salt, and rice in a pan. Simmer the mixture for twenty minutes until the rice turns fluffy. Drain and keep aside.

2. Heat oil in a pan. Chop the potatoes into small pieces and slice the onions in rings. Add the potatoes along with the onions to the pan. Add pepper and salt for seasoning; toss the mixture for five minutes. Keep aside.

3. Prepare the beans in a saucepan over a medium flame.

4. For making the slaw, mix lime juice and avocado in a bowl. Mash the avocado and mix. Add jalapeno, cabbage, and toss for combining. Add pepper and salt for seasoning.

5. Add cilantro and lime juice to the rice and combine using a fork.

6. Warm the tortillas in a pan or microwave for twenty seconds.

7. Add the prepared fillings to the tortillas in order of your choice and top with salsa; add sliced avocado from the top. Roll the tortillas and slice in half.

8. Serve with extra black beans and potatoes by the side.

Gingerbread Waffles

Total Prep & Cooking Time: Fifteen minutes

Yields: Six servings

Nutrition Facts: Calories: 170 | Protein: 4.2g | Carbs: 27.3g | Fat: 4.7g | Fiber: 3.9g

Ingredients:

- One cup of flour
- One tbsp. of flax seeds (ground)

- Two tsps. of baking powder
- One-fourth tsp. of each
    - Salt
    - Baking soda
- One tsp. of cinnamon (ground)
- One and a half tsps. of ginger (ground)
- Four tbsps. of brown sugar
- One cup of any non-dairy milk
- Two tbsps. of apple cider vinegar
- Two tbsps. of molasses
- One and a half tbsps. of olive oil

Method:

1. Preheat a waffle iron and grease it.
2. Put the dry ingredients in a mixing bowl and combine well.
3. Combine the wet ingredients in a medium mixing bowl or jug. Mix well until properly combined.
4. Add the mixture of wet ingredients into the dry mixture and mix well. The batter needs to be thick. In case the batter is excessively thick, you can add two tbsps. of non-dairy milk to the batter and mix.
5. Pour the batter in batches in the waffle iron and cook until steam stops to come out from the sides.
6. Open the waffle iron and take out the waffle carefully.
7. Serve warm.

Green Chickpeas And Toast

Total Prep & Cooking Time: Thirty minutes

Yields: Two servings

Nutrition Facts: Calories: 189 | Protein: 11.3g | Carbs: 27.1g | Fat: 3.2g | Fiber: 9.3g

Ingredients:

- Two tbsps. of olive oil
- Three shallots (diced)
- One-fourth tsp. of paprika (smoked)
- Two cloves of garlic (diced)
- Half tsp. of each
    - Sweet paprika
    - Salt
    - Cinnamon
    - Sugar
- Black pepper (according to taste)
- Two tomatoes (skinned)
- Two cups of chickpeas (cooked)
- Four crusty bread slices

Method:

1. Take a medium pan and heat oil in it.

2. Add the diced shallots to the oil and stir-fry. Add garlic to the pan. Cook for five minutes until shallots turn translucent.

3. Add spices to the pan and combine well with garlic and shallots. Stir for two minutes.

4. Add the tomatoes to the pan and squash them using a spoon or spatula. Add four tbsps. of water to the pan and simmer for twelve minutes.

5. Add cooked chickpeas and mix well. Add pepper, sugar, and salt.

6. Serve the cooked chickpeas on bread slices.

Asparagus And Tomato Quiche

Total Prep & Cooking Time: One hour and twenty minutes

Yields: Eight servings

Nutrition Facts: Calories: 219 | Protein: 4.1g | Carbs: 20.6g | Fat: 11.7g | Fiber: 3g

Ingredients:

- Two cups of flour
- Half tsp. of salt
- Half cup of non-dairy butter
- Two tbsps. of water (ice cold)

For filling:

- One tbsp. of coconut oil
- One cup of asparagus (chopped)
- One-fourth cup of onion (minced)
- Three tbsps. of each
    - Sun-dried tomatoes (chopped)
    - Nutritional yeast
    - Basil (chopped)
- One block of tofu (firm)
- One tbsp. of each
    - Flour
    - Non-dairy milk

- One tsp. of each
    - Minced onion (dehydrated)
    - Mustard
- Two tsps. of lemon juice
- Half tsp. of each
    - Salt
    - Turmeric
    - Liquid smoke

Method:

1. Spray a pie pan with oil and keep aside. Preheat your oven at 180 degrees Celsius.
2. Mix salt along with flour in a bowl. Add non-dairy butter along with cold water to the flour. Knead the dough on a working surface.
3. Press the dough on the pan. Bake the dough in the preheated oven for ten minutes.
4. Heat some oil in a pan and start adding asparagus, tomato, and onion—Cook for three minutes.
5. Combine onion, tofu, yeast, flour, non-dairy milk, lemon juice, liquid smoke, and salt in a blender.
6. Combine the mixture of asparagus with the tofu mixture.
7. Add the filling on the baked crust and smoothen the top.
8. Bake for half an hour.
9. Serve warm.

Breakfast Bowl

Total Prep & Cooking Time: One hour and twenty-five minutes

Yields: Two servings

Nutrition Facts: Calories: 350 | Protein: 7.2g | Carbs: 54g | Fat: 11.3g | Fiber: 9.3g

Ingredients:

- Two small sweet potatoes
- Cinnamon (ground, according to taste)
- Two tbsps. of each
    - Chopped nuts
    - Raisins
    - Almond butter

Method:

1. Preheat your oven at 180/160 degrees Celsius. Wash the potatoes and dry them using a kitchen towel. Use a fork for poking holes in the potatoes and wrap them using aluminum foil. Bake the potatoes for eighty minutes. Allow the potatoes to cool down before peeling.
2. Peel the baked potatoes and mash them with cinnamon.
3. Top with chopped nuts and raisins. Drizzle some almond butter from the top and serve.

Tofu Pancakes

Total Prep & Cooking Time: Twenty minutes

Yields: Six servings

Nutrition Facts: Calories: 370 | Protein: 11.2g | Carbs: 46.3g | Fat: 13.2g | Fiber: 7.9g

Ingredients:

- Fifty grams of Brazil nuts
- Three bananas (sliced)
- Three-hundred grams of raspberries
- Maple syrup (for serving)

For batter:

- Four-hundred grams of firm tofu
- Two tsps. of each
    - Lemon juice
    - Vanilla extract
- Four-hundred ml of almond milk
- One tbsp. of vegetable oil
- Two cups of buckwheat flour
- Four tbsps. of sugar
- Two tsps. of mixed spice (ground)
- One tbsp. of baking powder

Method:

1. Preheat your oven at 160 degrees Celsius. Cook the nuts by scattering them in a tray for five minutes. Chop the nuts.

2. Add vanilla, tofu, almond milk, and lemon juice in a deep bowl; blend the mixture using a stick blender. Add oil to the mixture and blend again.

3. Take a large bowl and combine the dry ingredients; add one tsp. of salt and combine. Add the mixture of tofu and combine.

4. Heat a pan and add one tsp. oil in it. Make sure that the pan is not excessively hot.

5. Use a large spoon for dropping three spoons of batter in the pan. Swirl the pan for making the pancake even—Cook for two minutes on each side. Repeat the same for the remaining batter.

6. Serve with berries, bananas, nuts, and drizzle some maple syrup from the top.

Chapter 2: Side Dish Recipes

Side dish plays a profound role in any proper meal. I have included some tasty and easy vegan side dish recipes in this section.

Baked Beans

Total Prep & Cooking Time: Five hours and twenty minutes

Yields: Ten servings

Nutrition Facts: Calories: 249 | Protein: 11.2g | Carbs: 45.3g | Fat: 2.9g | Fiber: 13.7g

Ingredients:

- Sixteen ounces of navy beans (dry)
- Six cups of water
- Two tbsps. of olive oil
- Two cups of sweet onion (chopped)
- One garlic clove (minced)
- Four cans of tomato sauce
- One-fourth cup of brown sugar
- Half cup of molasses
- Three tbsps. of cider vinegar
- Three bay leaves
- One tsp. of mustard (dry)
- One-fourth tsp. of each
    - Black pepper (ground)
    - Nutmeg (ground)
    - Cinnamon (ground)

Method:

1. Add water and beans in a pot and boil the mixture. Lower the flame and cook for one hour. Cook until the beans are tender. Drain the beans and keep aside.

2. Preheat your oven to 160 degrees Celsius.

3. Take an iron skillet and heat oil in it. Add onions in the oil. Cook for two minutes. Add garlic to the pan.

4. Combine the onion mixture with the cooked beans. Add tomato sauce, molasses, vinegar, brown sugar, pepper, bay leaves, cinnamon, mustard, and nutmeg. Mix well.

5. Cover the dish and bake for three hours. Stir in between.

6. Remove the cover and bake for forty minutes.

Baked Potato Wedges

Total Prep & Cooking Time: Fifty-five minutes

Yields: Four servings

Nutrition Facts: Calories: 234 | Protein: 5.1g | Carbs: 42.6g | Fat: 4.3g | Fiber: 8.9g

Ingredients:

- One tbsp. of olive oil
- Eight sweet potatoes (sliced into quarters)
- Half tsp. of paprika

Method:

1. Preheat your oven at 160/180 degrees Celsius.
2. Grease a baking sheet with cooking spray.
3. Combine potatoes and paprika in a bowl. Add the potatoes to the baking sheet.
4. Bake for forty minutes.
5. Serve warm.

Black Beans And Quinoa

Total Prep & Cooking Time: Fifty minutes

Yields: Ten servings

Nutrition Facts: Calories: 143 | Protein: 8.7g | Carbs: 25.6g | Fat: 1.2g | Fiber: 8.7g

Ingredients:

- One tsp. of vegetable oil
- One large onion (chopped)
- Three garlic cloves (chopped)
- Three-fourth cup of quinoa
- Two cups of vegetable stock
- One tsp. of cumin (ground)
- One-fourth tsp. of cayenne powder
- One cup of corn kernels (frozen)
- Two cans of black beans (rinsed)
- Half cup of cilantro (chopped)
- Pepper and salt (according to taste)

Method:

1. Take a medium pan and heat oil in it. Add garlic and onion to the pan. Cook for ten minutes until browned.

2. Add quinoa to the pan and mix well. Cover the mixture with vegetable stock. Season with salt, pepper, and cayenne. Boil the mixture. Cover the pan and simmer for twenty minutes until quinoa gets tender.

3. Add the corn kernels to the pan and simmer for five minutes.

4. Add cilantro and black beans to the mixture.

5. Serve hot.

Roasted Lemon Garlic Broccoli

Total Prep & Cooking Time: Twenty-five minutes

Yields: Six servings

Nutrition Facts: Calories: 48.3 | Protein: 3g | Carbs: 6.9g | Fat: 1.8g | Fiber: 3g

Ingredients:

- Two heads of broccoli (separate the florets)
- Two tsps. of olive oil (extra virgin)
- One tsp. of salt
- Half tsp. of black pepper (ground)
- One garlic clove (minced)
- One-fourth tsp. of lemon juice

Method:

1. Preheat your oven at 180/200 degrees Celsius.
2. Toss the florets of broccoli with olive oil in a bowl. Add pepper, garlic, and salt. Spread the coated broccoli florets on a baking sheet.
3. Bake for twenty minutes.
4. Add lemon juice from the top and serve warm.

Spicy Tofu

Total Prep & Cooking Time: Twenty minutes

Yields: Four servings

Nutrition Facts: Calories: 305.2 | Protein: 20.1g | Carbs: 15.4g | Fat: 19.3g | Fiber: 5.2g

Ingredients:

- Three tbsps. of peanut oil
- One red onion (sliced)
- One pound of tofu (firm, cubed)
- One bell pepper (sliced)
- One chili pepper (chopped)
- Three garlic cloves (crushed)
- One-third cup of hot water
- Two tbsps. of each
    - Soy sauce
    - White vinegar
- One tsp. of cornstarch
- One tbsp. of each
    - Red pepper flakes (crushed)
    - Brown sugar

Method:

1. Take a wok and heat oil in it. Add the tofu to the oil and keep cooking until browned. Add bell pepper, onion, garlic, and chili pepper. Mix well and cook for five minutes.

2. Whisk vinegar, soy sauce, red pepper flakes, brown sugar, and cornstarch in a bowl.

3. Add the mixture of vinegar to the wok and toss well for coating. Simmer the mixture for five minutes.

4. Serve hot.

Spanish Rice

Total Prep & Cooking Time: Forty minutes

Yields: Four servings

Nutrition Facts: Calories: 267.2 | Protein: 4.7g | Carbs: 42.7g | Fat: 5.6g | Fiber: 3g

Ingredients:

- Two tbsps. of vegetable oil
- One cup of white rice (uncooked)
- One onion (chopped)
- Half bell pepper (chopped)
- Two cups of water
- One can of green chilies and diced tomatoes
- Two tsps. of chili powder
- One tsp. of salt

Method:

1. Take a deep skillet and heat oil in it. Add onion, rice, and bell pepper to the skillet. Sauté until onions are soft and rice gets browned.
2. Add tomatoes and water to the skillet. Add salt and chili powder.
3. Simmer the mixture for thirty minutes and cover the skillet.
4. Serve hot.

Pepper And Lemon Pasta

Total Prep & Cooking Time: Twenty minutes

Yields: Eight servings

Nutrition Facts: Calories: 232.8 | Protein: 8.5g | Carbs: 41g | Fat: 4.6g | Fiber: 3.6g

Ingredients:

- One pound of spaghetti
- Two tbsps. of olive oil
- One tbsp. of basil (dried) Three tbsps. of lemon juice
- Black pepper (ground, according to taste)

Method:

1. Take a large pot and boil water in it with light salt. Add the pasta to the pot and cook for ten minutes. Drain the pasta.
2. Combine lemon juice, black pepper, lemon juice, and basil in a bowl.
3. Add the lemon mixture to the cooked pasta and toss it properly.
4. Serve cold or hot.

Chapter 3: High Protein Recipes

The vegan diet is rich in proteins, as it is mainly composed of plant compounds. Here are some easy to make vegan high protein recipes for you.

Kale Salad With Spicy Tempeh Bits And Chickpeas

Total Prep & Cooking Time: Forty-five minutes

Yields: Four servings

Nutrition Facts: Calories: 473 | Protein: 25g | Carbs: 41g | Fat: 27.1g | Fiber: 17.3g

Ingredients:

- Eight ounces of tempeh
- One-fourth cup of vegetable oil
- One-fourth tsp. of salt
- Two tsps. of each
  - Garlic powder
  - Onion powder
  - Sweet paprika
- One tsp. of each
  - Lemon pepper
  - Chili powder
- One-eighth tsp. of cayenne powder

For salad:

- 400 grams of kale (chopped)
- One cup of carrots (shredded)
- One can of chickpeas
- Two tbsps. of sesame seeds

For dressing:

- Half cup of rice vinegar
- One-fourth cup of soy sauce
- Two tbsps. of sesame oil
- One tbsp. of ginger (grated)

Method:

1. Boil water with salt in a large pot. Blanch the kale for thirty seconds. Wash blanched kale under running water. Squeeze out excess water from kale and keep aside.
2. Preheat your oven to 180 degrees Celsius.
3. Mix all the spices for tempeh in a mixing bowl.
4. Cut tempeh into very thin slices.
5. Dip each tempeh slice in oil and arrange them on a baking sheet. Line the tray using parchment paper. Sprinkle the mix of spices from the top. Coat well.
6. Bake tempeh for twenty minutes until crispy and brown in color.
7. Take a large bowl and combine the listed ingredients for the salad.
8. Combine the ingredients of dressing in a jar and shake well.
9. Pour the dressing over the prepared salad. Toss well. Make sure the salad gets coated properly with the dressing.
10. Crumble the slices of tempeh over the salad.

Protein Bars

Total Prep & Cooking Time: One hour and twenty minutes

Yields: Ten servings

Nutrition Facts: Calories: 292 | Protein: 13g | Carbs: 37.9g | Fat: 9.6g | Fiber: 2.3g

Ingredients:

For crust:

- Two cups of oat flour
- Six apricots (dried)
- One-fourth cup of each
    - Brown rice syrup
    - Cocoa powder

For layer:

- One cup of oat flour
- Half cup of each
    - Vegan protein powder (chocolate)
    - Rolled oats
- One-fourth tsp. of salt
- Two tbsps. of each
    - Hemp seeds (hulled)

    - Chia seeds
- Half cup of almond butter
- One-fourth cup of any vegan sweetener
- One cup of coconut milk
- One tbsp. flax seeds (ground)

Method:

1. Combine all the ingredients for the crust in a blender. Keep the dough aside.
2. Take a large bowl and mix the dry ingredients for the next layer. You can use a fork for proper mixing.
3. Mix water and flax in a bowl and keep aside until it turns into a gel.
4. Add almond butter, sweetener, coconut milk, and flax gel to the mixture of dry ingredients. Use a fork for mixing properly.
5. Pour the mixture in a food processor and blend well for making it smooth.
6. Use parchment paper for lining a baking sheet. Add the crust to the sheet and press the crust out. Add the next layer on the crust and evenly spread it out.
7. Put the baking sheet in the freezer for one hour.
8. Serve by cutting bars of your desired size and shape.

Tofu And Spinach Scramble

Total Prep & Cooking Time: Thirty minutes

Yields: Two servings

Nutrition Facts: Calories: 319 | Protein: 22.1g | Carbs: 11.4g | Fat: 22g | Fiber: 6.5g

Ingredients:

- Fourteen ounces of tofu (firm, cut into cubes of half-inch)
- Half tsp. of turmeric (ground)
- Black pepper and kosher salt (to taste)
- One-eighth tsp. of cayenne powder (ground)
- Two tbsps. of olive oil (extra virgin)
- Three scallions (sliced)
- Five ounces of spinach (chopped)
- Two tsps. of lemon juice
- One cup of grape tomatoes (halved)
- Half cup of basil (chopped)

Method:

1. Mix turmeric, tofu, one-fourth tsp. of salt, cayenne, and half tsp. of black pepper in a bowl. Toss the ingredients for mixing properly.

2. Take a large skillet and heat oil in it; add the scallions and stir for about one minute. Add tofu mixture and cook for five minutes until the tofu gets browned.

3. Add lemon juice, spinach, and half tsp. of salt to the tofu. Cook for one minute until the spinach wilts. Add tomatoes and stir for one minute.

4. Remove the skillet from heat and add basil.

5. Serve hot.

Vegan Tacos

Total Prep & Cooking Time: Twenty minutes

Yields: Six servings

Nutrition Facts: Calories: 402 | Protein: 29g | Carbs: 71.2g | Fat: 5.4g | Fiber: 20.3g

Ingredients:

- One tsp. of vegetable oil

- Half onion (diced)
- Two tsps. of jalapeno (chopped)
- Twelve ounces of soy chorizo (remove the casing)
- Sixteen ounces of refried black beans
- Twelve tortillas (corn)
- Cilantro (chopped)

Method:

1. Take a skillet and heat oil in it. Add onion and jalapeno to the skillet—Cook for ten minutes. Add chorizo and cook for five minutes.
2. Take a small pan and cook the beans on low heat.
3. Arrange two tortillas for making six tacos in total.
4. Spread the beans on the tortillas; top the beans with the mixture of chorizo. Serve with cilantro from the top.

Grilled Tofu Steaks And Spinach Salad

Total Prep & Cooking Time: One hour

Yields: Two servings

Nutrition Facts: Calories: 154 | Protein: 22g | Carbs: 8g | Fat: 11.3g | Fiber: 9.3g

Ingredients:

For tofu steak:

- Half block of tofu (firm)
- One tbsp. of soy sauce
- One tsp. of each
    - Miso paste
    - Tomato paste
    - Olive oil
- Half tsp. of maple syrup
- One-fourth cup of breadcrumbs

For spinach salad:

- Two cups of baby spinach
- One tbsp. of each
    - Olive oil (extra virgin)
    - Pine nuts
    - Lemon juice
- Pinch of salt
- Pinch of black pepper (ground)

Method:

1. Cut the tofu block in half and squeeze out any excess water. Make sure you do not break the block of tofu. Use paper towels for drying the tofu.
2. Cut the tofu in size and shape of your choice.
3. Take a small mixing bowl and combine tomato paste, soy sauce, olive oil, sesame, miso paste, and maple syrup. Mix until the sauce is smooth.
4. Spread breadcrumbs in a shallow dish.
5. Dip the pieces of tofu in the prepared sauce and then coat them in breadcrumbs. Repeat for the remaining tofu.
6. Grease a grill pan with some olive oil. Add the tofu steaks and cook for fifteen minutes on each side. Cook until both sides are browned.
7. For the salad, mix the listed ingredients in a medium-sized mixing bowl. Toss the ingredients properly.
8. Serve the tofu steaks with spinach salad by the side.

Corn, Quinoa, And Edamame Salad

Total Prep & Cooking Time: Two hours and ten minutes

Yields: Four servings

Nutrition Facts: Calories: 130 | Protein: 18g | Carbs: 13g | Fat: 5.8g | Fiber: 3.1g

Ingredients:

- One cup of corn kernels (frozen)
- Two cups of shelled edamame
- Half cup of cooked quinoa
- One green onion (sliced)
- Half sweet bell pepper (diced)
- Two tbsps. of cilantro (chopped)
- One and a half tbsps. of olive oil
- One tbsp. of each
    - Lime juice
    - Lemon juice
- One-fourth tsp. of each
    - Salt
    - Thyme (dried)
    - Chili powder
    - Black pepper (ground)

Method:

1. Boil corn and edamame in water with a little bit of salt. Drain and keep aside.

2. Take a bowl and mix corn, edamame, quinoa, bell pepper, green onion, and cilantro.

3. Whisk together lemon juice, olive oil, lime juice, chili powder, salt, thyme, and black pepper in a small bowl.

4. Pour the dressing all over the salad. Mix well.

5. Chill in the refrigerator for two hours.

Lentil Soup

Total Prep & Cooking Time: Fifty-five minutes

Yields: Six servings

Nutrition Facts: Calories: 230 | Protein: 9.2g | Carbs: 31.2g | Fat: 8.6g | Fiber: 11.3g

Ingredients:

- Two tbsps. of olive oil (extra virgin)
- One onion (diced)

- Two carrots (diced)
- Two stalks of celery (diced)
- One bell pepper (diced)
- Three garlic cloves (minced)
- One tbsp. of cumin
- One-fourth tsp. of paprika
- One tsp. of oregano
- Two cups of tomatoes (diced)
- Two cans of green lentils (rinsed)
- Eight cups of vegetable stock
- Half tsp. of salt
- Cilantro (for garnishing)
- One ripe avocado (diced)

Method:

1. Heat some oil in a pot. Start adding bell pepper, onion, carrots, and celery to the pot. Sauté the veggies for five minutes until tender; add paprika, cumin, garlic, and oregano. Mix well.

2. Add chilies, tomatoes, stock, salt, and lentils; simmer the mixture for forty minutes. Add pepper and salt according to taste.

3. Serve with avocado and cilantro from the top.

Chapter 4: Dessert Recipes

Everyone loves to have some dessert after having their meals. Desserts can be vegan too. So in this section, I have included some tasty dessert recipes that you can make easily.

Chocolate Pudding

Total Prep & Cooking Time: Forty-five minutes

Yields: Two servings

Nutrition Facts: Calories: 265.1 | Protein: 8.3g | Carbs: 52.2g | Fat: 4.6g | Fiber: 4.9g

Ingredients:

- Three tbsps. of cornstarch
- Two tbsps. of water
- Two cups of soy milk
- One-fourth tsp. of vanilla extract
- One-fourth cup of white sugar
- One cup of cocoa powder

Method:

1. Take a small bowl and mix water and cornstarch for forming a fine paste.
2. Take a saucepan and heat it over medium flame. Add soy milk, sugar, vanilla, a mixture of cornstarch, and cocoa. Stir the mixture until it starts boiling. Keep cooking until the mixture gets thick.
3. Allow the pudding to cool for five minutes.
4. Chill in the fridge for twenty minutes.

Orange Cake

Total Prep & Cooking Time: Forty-five minutes

Yields: Sixteen servings

Nutrition Facts: Calories: 147.3 | Protein: 1.9g | Carbs: 21.6g | Fat: 6.3g | Fiber: 0.8g

Ingredients:

- One large-sized onion (peeled)
- Two cups of flour
- One cup of white sugar
- Half cup of vegetable oil
- One and a half tsps. of baking soda
- Half tsp. of salt

Method:

1. Preheat your oven to 190 degrees Celsius. Grease a baking pan with some oil.
2. Blend the orange in a food processor until it gets completely liquefied.
3. Combine orange juice, sugar, flour, vegetable oil, baking soda, and salt. Pour the cake batter into prepared baking pan.
4. Bake the cake for thirty minutes.

Notes:

- In case you do not want to make orange juice at home, you can use orange juice from the store.
- This cake can be converted into a plain cake by omitting orange juice and using soy milk along with rice milk.

Pumpkin Tofu Pie

Total Prep & Cooking Time: Two hours

Yields: Eight servings

Nutrition Facts: Calories: 229.3 | Protein: 4.7g | Carbs: 33.6g | Fat: 8.6g | Fiber: 3.7g

Ingredients

- Ten ounces of silken tofu (drained)
- One can of pumpkin puree
- Three-fourth cup of white sugar
- Half tsp. of salt
- One tsp. of cinnamon (ground)
- One-fourth tsp. of ginger (ground)
- One-eighth tsp. of cloves (ground)
- One pie crust (unbaked)

Method:

1. Preheat the oven at 220/230 degrees Celsius.
2. Add pumpkin puree, tofu, cinnamon, salt, sugar, clove, and ginger in a food processor. Blend the ingredients until smooth.
3. Pour over the blended mixture into the crust.
4. Bake the pie for fifteen minutes and then reduce the temperature to 175 degrees Celsius. Bake again for forty minutes.
5. Let the pie cool down.
6. Serve at room temperature.

Note: If you are allergic to certain ingredients, check the ingredients of the pie crust.

Vegan Brownie

Total Prep & Cooking Time: Fifty minutes

Yields: Sixteen servings

Nutrition Facts: Calories: 254.3 | Protein: 2.6g | Carbs: 38.3g | Fat: 13.6g | Fiber: 2.8g

Ingredients:

- Two cups of flour
- Two cups of white sugar
- Three-fourth cup of cocoa powder (unsweetened)
- One tsp. of baking powder
- Half tsp. of salt
- One cup of each
    - Vegetable oil
    - Water
- One and a half tsps. of vanilla extract

Method:

1. Preheat your oven at 160/175 degrees Celsius.
2. Take a large bowl and combine sugar, flour, cocoa powder, salt, and baking powder. Add vegetable oil, vanilla extract, and water to the mixture. Mix well for making a smooth batter.
3. Spread the brownie mix in a baking pan.
4. Bake the brownie for thirty minutes.
5. Allow the brownie to cool for ten minutes.
6. Cut in squares and serve.

Vegan Cupcake

Total Prep & Cooking Time: Twenty-five minutes

Yields: Eighteen servings

Nutrition Facts: Calories: 150.2 | Protein: 1.9g | Carbs: 21.6g | Fat: 6.3g | Fiber: 0.9g

Ingredients:

- One tbsp. of cider vinegar
- Two cups of almond milk
- Two and a half cups of flour
- One cup of white sugar
- Two tsps. of baking powder
- Half tsp. of each
    - Salt
    - Baking soda
    - Coconut oil (warmed)
- One and a half tsps. of vanilla extract

Method:

1. Preheat the oven at 160/175 degrees Celsius. Grease eighteen muffin cups using some oil.

2. Mix cider vinegar and almond milk in a bowl. Allow it to stand for five minutes until the mixture gets curdled.

3. Take a bowl and combine sugar, salt, baking powder, flour, and baking soda.

4. Take another bowl and combine coconut oil, vanilla, and almond milk mixture. Add this mixture to the mixture of dry ingredients.

5. Divide the batter into muffin cups—Bake for twenty minutes.

6. Allow the cupcakes to sit for ten minutes.

7. Serve with the desired frosting from the top.

Vanilla Cake

Total Prep & Cooking Time: Fifty minutes

Yields: Eight servings

Nutrition Facts: Calories: 277.9 | Protein: 3.5g | Carbs: 44.2g | Fat: 9.2g | Fiber: 0.9g

Ingredients:

- One cup of soy milk
- One tbsp. of apple cider vinegar
- One and a half cup of flour
- One cup of white sugar
- One tsp. of each
    - Baking powder
    - Baking soda
- Half tsp. of salt
- One-third cup of canola oil
- One-fourth tsp. of almond extract
- One tbsp. of vanilla extract
- One-fourth cup of water

Method:

1. Preheat your oven at about 160/175 degrees Celsius. Grease a baking pan with some oil.

2. Mix vinegar and soy milk in a large cup.

3. Combine sugar, flour, salt, baking soda, and baking powder in a bowl.

4. Add lemon juice, canola oil, vanilla extract, almond extract, and water to the mixture of soy milk. Stir the mixture of soy milk into the mixture of flour. Mix well until there is no lump.

5. Pour the cake batter in the baking dish.

6. Bake in the preheated oven for thirty-five minutes.

Miracle Fudge

Total Prep & Cooking Time: One hour and ten minutes

Yields: Twenty-four servings

Nutrition Facts: Calories: 77.3 | Protein: 0.9g | Carbs: 4.9g | Fat: 6.2g | Fiber: 1.2g

Ingredients:

- Half cup of cocoa (unsweetened)
- One cup of maple syrup
- One tsp. of vanilla extract
- One pinch of salt
- One-third cup of each
    - Chopped walnuts
    - Coconut oil (melted)
- One tsp. of cocoa powder (unsweetened, for dusting)

Method

1. Add half cup of cocoa powder in a bowl along with maple syrup; give it a stir. Add vanilla extract and salt. Add melted coconut oil and combine well.

2. Add walnuts in a pan and toast them for one minute.

3. Add the toasted walnuts to the fudge. Mix well.

4. Pour the mixture of fudge into a silicone mold. Smoothen the top.

5. Wrap the silicone mold using plastic wrap and put it in the freezer for thirty minutes. Take out the fudge pieces from the mold and dust with cocoa powder from the top.

6. Serve cold.

Chapter 5: Sauces & Dips Recipes

Sauces and dips are important components of any meal that can make the food tastier. Here are some vegan sauces and dips recipes for you.

Tomato Jam

Total Prep & Cooking Time: Forty-five minutes

Yields: One full cup

Nutrition Facts: Calories: 34 | Protein: 0.2g | Carbs: 8.6g | Fat: 0.1g | Fiber: 0.2g

Ingredients:

- Two pounds of plum tomatoes
- One-fourth cup of coconut sugar
- Half tsp. of salt
- One-fourth tsp. of paprika
- One tsp. of vinegar (white wine)
- Black pepper (to taste)

Method:

1. Take a large pot and boil water in it; add the tomatoes to the water and boil for one minute. Remove the tomatoes and put them in an ice-water bath.

2. Peel the blanched tomatoes and chop them.

3. Add chopped tomatoes in a pot over a medium flame. Add sugar and stir the mixture—Cook for ten minutes.

4. Add pepper, salt, and paprika. Simmer for ten minutes until the jam thickens.

5. Remove from heat and add white wine vinegar. Serve with crackers, burgers, toasts, etc.

Walnut Kale Pesto

Total Prep & Cooking Time: Thirty minutes

Yields: One small bowl

Nutrition Facts: Calories: 240 | Protein: 3.6g | Carbs: 2.6g | Fat: 22.3g | Fiber: 0.8g

Ingredients:

- Half bunch of kale (chopped)
- Half cup of walnuts (chopped)
- Two garlic cloves (minced)
- One-fourth cup of yeast
- One cup of olive oil
- Three tbsps. of lemon juice
- Pepper and salt (for seasoning)

Method:

1. Take a pot and boil water in it. Add kale to the pot with one tsp. of salt—Cook for five minutes.
2. Add kale, garlic, walnuts, olive oil, yeast, along with lemon juice in a food processor. Add pepper and salt according to your taste. Blend well.

Ranch Dressing

Total Prep & Cooking Time: Thirty minutes

Yields: One small bowl

Nutrition Facts: Calories: 92 | Protein: 0.1g | Carbs: 1g | Fat: 9.1g | Fiber: 0.4g

Ingredients:

- One cup of vegan mayo
- Half tsp. of each
    - Onion powder
    - Garlic powder
- One-fourth tsp. of black pepper (ground)
- Two tsps. of parsley (chopped)
- One tbsp. of dill (chopped)
- Half cup of soy milk (unsweetened)

Method:

1. Mix the listed ingredients in a medium mixing bowl.
2. If you want the dressing to be thin, add a bit of almond milk. Allow the dressing to sit for a few minutes.
3. Chill the prepared dressing.

Notes:

- You can serve the dressing with any savory snacks, sandwiches, quick-bites, salads, etc.
- You can store the leftover dressing in the fridge for two days.
- You can add some ground nuts for enhancing the flavor.

PART III

Smoothie Diet Recipes

The smoothie diet is all about replacing some of your meals with smoothies that are loaded with veggies and fruits. It has been found that the smoothie diet is very helpful in losing weight along with excess fat. The ingredients of the smoothies will vary, but they will focus mainly on vegetables and fruits. The best part about the smoothie diet is that there is no need to count your calorie intake and less food tracking. The diet is very low in calories and is also loaded with phytonutrients.

Apart from weight loss, there are various other benefits of the smoothie diet. It can help you to stay full for a longer time as most smoothies are rich in fiber. It can also help you to control your cravings as smoothies are full of flavor and nutrients. Whenever you feel like snacking, just prepare a smoothie, and you are good to go. Also, smoothies can aid in digestion as they are rich in important minerals and vitamins. Fruits such as mango are rich in carotenoids that can help in improving your skin quality. As the smoothie diet is mainly based on veggies and fruits, it can detoxify your body.

In this section, you will find various recipes of smoothies that you can include in your smoothie diet.

Chapter 1: Fruit Smoothies

The best way of having fruits is by making smoothies. Fruit smoothies can help you start your day with loads of nutrients so that you can remain energetic throughout the day. Here are some easy-to-make fruit smoothie recipes that you can enjoy during any time of the day.

Quick Fruit Smoothie

Total Prep & Cooking Time: Fifteen minutes

Yields: Four servings

Nutrition Facts: Calories: 115.2 | Protein: 1.2g | Carbs: 27.2g | Fat: 0.5g | Fiber: 3.6g

Ingredients

- One cup of strawberries
- One banana (cut in chunks)
- Two peaches
- Two cups of ice
- One cup of orange and mango juice

Method:

1. Add banana, strawberries, and peaches in a blender.
2. Blend until frothy and smooth.
3. Add the orange and mango juice and blend again. Add ice for adjusting the consistency and blend for two minutes.
4. Divide the smoothie in glasses and serve with mango chunks from the top.

Triple Threat Smoothie

Total Prep & Cooking Time: Ten minutes

Yields: Four servings

Nutrition Facts: Calories: 132.2 | Protein: 3.4g | Carbs: 27.6g | Fat: 1.3g | Fiber: 2.7g

Ingredients

- One kiwi (sliced)
- One banana (chopped)
- One cup of each
    - Ice cubes
    - Strawberries
- Half cup of blueberries
- One-third cup of orange juice
- Eight ounces of peach yogurt

Method:

1. Add kiwi, strawberries, and bananas in a food processor.
2. Blend until smooth.
3. Add the blueberries along with orange juice. Blend again for two minutes.
4. Add peach yogurt and ice cubes. Give it a pulse.
5. Pour the prepared smoothie in smoothie glasses and serve with blueberry chunks from the top.

Tropical Smoothie

Total Prep & Cooking Time: Fifteen minutes

Yields: Two servings

Nutrition Facts: Calories: 127.3 | Protein: 1.6g | Carbs: 30.5g | Fat: 0.7g | Fiber: 4.2g

Ingredients

- One mango (seeded)
- One papaya (cubed)
- Half cup of strawberries
- One-third cup of orange juice
- Five ice cubes

Method:

1. Add mango, strawberries, and papaya in a blender. Blend the ingredients until smooth.
2. Add ice cubes and orange juice for adjusting the consistency.
3. Blend again.
4. Serve with strawberry chunks from the top.

Fruit and Mint Smoothie

Total Prep & Cooking Time: Fifteen minutes

Yields: Two servings

Nutrition Facts: Calories: 90.3 | Protein: 0.7g | Carbs: 21.4g | Fat: 0.4g | Fiber: 2.5g

Ingredients

- One-fourth cup of each
  - Applesauce (unsweetened)
  - Red grapes (seedless, frozen)
- One tbsp. of lime juice
- Three strawberries (frozen)
- One cup of pineapple cubes
- Three mint leaves

Method:

1. Add grapes, lime juice, and applesauce in a blender. Blend the ingredients until frothy and smooth.
2. Add pineapple cubes, mint leaves, and frozen strawberries in the blender. Pulse the ingredients for a few times until the pineapple and strawberries are crushed.
3. Serve with mint leaves from the top.

Banana Smoothie

Total Prep & Cooking Time: Ten minutes

Yields: Four servings

Nutrition Facts: Calories: 122.6 | Protein: 1.3g | Carbs: 34.6g | Fat: 0.4g | Fiber: 2.2g

Ingredients

- Three bananas (sliced)
- One cup of fresh pineapple juice
- One tbsp. of honey
- Eight cubes of ice

Method:

1. Combine the bananas and pineapple juice in a blender.
2. Blend until smooth.
3. Add ice cubes along with honey.
4. Blend for two minutes.
5. Serve immediately.

Dragon Fruit Smoothie

Total Prep & Cooking Time: Twenty minutes

Yields: Four servings

Nutrition Facts: Calories: 147.6 | Protein: 5.2g | Carbs: 21.4g | Fat: 6.4g | Fiber: 2.9g

Ingredients

- One-fourth cup of almonds
- Two tbsps. of shredded coconut
- One tsp. of chocolate chips
- One cup of yogurt
- One dragon fruit (chopped)
- Half cup of pineapple cubes
- One tbsp. of honey

Method:

1. Add almonds, dragon fruit, coconut, and chocolate chips in a high power blender. Blend until smooth.
2. Add yogurt, pineapple, and honey. Blend well.
3. Serve with chunks of dragon fruit from the top.

Kefir Blueberry Smoothie

Total Prep & Cooking Time: Fifteen minutes

Yields: Two servings

Nutrition Facts: Calories: 304.2 | Protein: 7.3g | Carbs: 41.3g | Fat: 13.2g | Fiber: 4.6g

Ingredients

- Half cup of kefir
- One cup of blueberries (frozen)
- Half banana (cubed)

- One tbsp. of almond butter
- Two tsps. of honey

Method:

1. Add blueberries, banana cubes, and kefir in a blender.
2. Blend until smooth.
3. Add honey and almond butter.
4. Pulse the smoothie for a few times.
5. Serve immediately.

Ginger Fruit Smoothie

Total Prep & Cooking Time: Fifteen minutes

Yields: Two servings

Nutrition Facts: Calories: 160.2 | Protein: 1.9g | Carbs: 41.3g | Fat: 0.7g | Fiber: 5.6g

Ingredients

- One-fourth cup of each
    - Blueberries (frozen)
    - Green grapes (seedless)
- Half cup of green apple (chopped)
- One cup of water
- Three strawberries
- One piece of ginger
- One tbsp. of agave nectar

Method:

1. Add blueberries, grapes, and water in a blender. Blend the ingredients.
2. Add green apple, strawberries, agave nectar, and ginger. Blend for making thick slushy.
3. Serve immediately.

Fruit Batido

Total Prep & Cooking Time: Fifteen minutes

Yields: Six servings

Nutrition Facts: Calories: 129.3 | Protein: 4.2g | Carbs: 17.6g | Fat: 4.6g | Fiber: 0.6g

Ingredients

- One can of evaporated milk
- One cup of papaya (chopped)
- One-fourth cup of white sugar
- One tsp. of vanilla extract
- One tsp. of cinnamon (ground)
- One tray of ice cubes

Method:

1. Add papaya, white sugar, cinnamon, and vanilla extract in a food processor. Blend the ingredients until smooth.
2. Add milk and ice cubes. Blend for making slushy.
3. Serve immediately.

Banana Peanut Butter Smoothie

Total Prep & Cooking Time: Ten minutes

Yields: Four servings

Nutrition Facts: Calories: 332 | Protein: 13.2g | Carbs: 35.3g | Fat: 17.8g | Fiber: 3.9g

Ingredients

- Two bananas (cubed)
- Two cups of milk
- Half cup of peanut butter
- Two tbsps. of honey
- Two cups of ice cubes

Method:

1. Add banana cubes and peanut butter in a blender. Blend for making a smooth paste.
2. Add milk, ice cubes, and honey. Blend the ingredients until smooth.
3. Serve with banana chunks from the top.

Chapter 2: Breakfast Smoothies

Smoothie forms an essential part of breakfast in the smoothie diet plan. Here are some breakfast smoothie recipes for you that can be included in your daily breakfast plan.

Berry Banana Smoothie

Total Prep & Cooking Time: Twenty minutes

Yields: Two servings

Nutrition Facts: Calories: 330 | Protein: 6.7g | Carbs: 56.3g | Fat: 13.2g | Fiber: 5.5g

Ingredients

- One cup of each
  - Strawberries
  - Peaches (cubed)
  - Apples (cubed)
- One banana (cubed)
- Two cups of vanilla ice cream
- Half cup of ice cubes
- One-third cup of milk

Method:

1. Place strawberries, peaches, banana, and apples in a blender. Pulse the ingredients.
2. Add milk, ice cream, and ice cubes. Blend the smoothie until frothy and smooth.
3. Serve with a scoop of ice cream from the top.

Berry Surprise

Total Prep & Cooking Time: Ten minutes

Yields: Two servings

Nutrition Facts: Calories: 164.2 | Protein: 1.2g | Carbs: 40.2g | Fat: 0.4g | Fiber: 4.8g

Ingredients

- One cup of strawberries
- Half cup of pineapple cubes
- One-third cup of raspberries
- Two tbsps. of limeade concentrate (frozen)

Method:

1. Combine pineapple cubes, strawberries, and raspberries in a food processor. Blend the ingredients until smooth.
2. Add the frozen limeade and blend again.
3. Divide the smoothie in glasses and serve immediately.

Coconut Matcha Smoothie

Total Prep & Cooking Time: Twenty minutes

Yields: Two servings

Nutrition Facts: Calories: 362 | Protein: 7.2g | Carbs: 70.1g | Fat: 8.7g | Fiber: 12.1g

Ingredients

- One large banana
- One cup of frozen mango cubes
- Two leaves of kale (torn)
- Three tbsps. of white beans (drained)
- Two tbsps. of shredded coconut (unsweetened)
- Half tsp. of matcha green tea (powder)
- Half cup of water

Method:

1. Add cubes of mango, banana, white beans, and kale in a blender. Blend all the ingredients until frothy and smooth.
2. Add shredded coconut, white beans, water, and green tea powder. Blend for thirty seconds.
3. Serve with shredded coconut from the top.

Cantaloupe Frenzy

Total Prep & Cooking Time: Ten minutes

Yields: Three servings

Nutrition Facts: Calories: 108.3 | Protein: 1.6g | Carbs: 26.2g | Fat: 0.2g | Fiber: 1.6g

Ingredients

- One cantaloupe (seeded, chopped)
- Three tbsps. of white sugar
- Two cups of ice cubes

Method:

1. Place the chopped cantaloupe along with white sugar in a blender. Puree the mixture.
2. Add cubes of ice and blend again.
3. Pour the smoothie in serving glasses. Serve immediately.

Berry Lemon Smoothie

Total Prep & Cooking Time: Ten minutes

Yields: Four servings

Nutrition Facts: Calories: 97.2 | Protein: 5.4g | Carbs: 19.4g | Fat: 0.4g | Fiber: 1.8g

Ingredients

- Eight ounces of blueberry yogurt
- One and a half cup of milk (skim)
- One cup of ice cubes
- Half cup of blueberries
- One-third cup of strawberries
- One tsp. of lemonade mix

Method:

1. Add blueberry yogurt, skim milk, blueberries, and strawberries in a food processor. Blend the ingredients until smooth.
2. Add lemonade mix and ice cubes. Pulse the mixture for making a creamy and smooth smoothie.
3. Divide the smoothie in glasses and serve.

Orange Glorious

Total Prep & Cooking Time: Ten minutes

Yields: Four servings

Nutrition Facts: Calories: 212 | Protein: 3.4g | Carbs: 47.3g | Fat: 1.5g | Fiber: 0.5g

Ingredients

- Six ounces of orange juice concentrate (frozen)
- One cup of each
  - Water
  - Milk
- Half cup of white sugar
- Twelve ice cubes
- One tsp. of vanilla extract

Method:

1. Combine orange juice concentrate, white sugar, milk, and water in a blender.
2. Add vanilla extract and ice cubes. Blend the mixture until smooth.
3. Pour the smoothie in glasses and enjoy!

Grapefruit Smoothie

Total Prep & Cooking Time: Ten minutes

Yields: Two servings

Nutrition Facts: Calories: 200.3 | Protein: 4.7g | Carbs: 46.3g | Fat: 1.2g | Fiber: 7.6g

Ingredients

- Three grapefruits (peeled)
- One cup of water
- Three ounces of spinach
- Six ice cubes
- Half-inch piece of ginger
- One tsp. of flax seeds

Method:

1. Combine spinach, grapefruit, and ginger in a high power blender. Blend until smooth.
2. Add water, flax seeds, and ice cubes. Blend smooth.
3. Pour the smoothie in glasses and serve.

Sour Smoothie

Total Prep & Cooking Time: Ten minutes

Yields: Two servings

Nutrition Facts: Calories: 102.6 | Protein: 2.3g | Carbs: 30.2g | Fat: 0.7g | Fiber: 7.9g

Ingredients

- One cup of ice cubes
- Two fruit limes (peeled)
- One orange (peeled)
- One lemon (peeled)
- One kiwi (peeled)
- One tsp. of honey

Method:

1. Add fruit limes, lemon, orange, and kiwi in a food processor. Blend until frothy and smooth.
2. Add cubes of ice and honey. Pulse the ingredients.
3. Divide the smoothie in glasses and enjoy!

Ginger Orange Smoothie

Total Prep & Cooking Time: Ten minutes

Yields: One serving

Nutrition Facts: Calories: 115.6 | Protein: 2.2g | Carbs: 27.6g | Fat: 1.3g | Fiber: 5.7g

Ingredients

- One large orange
- Two carrots (peeled, cut in chunks)
- Half cup of each
    - Red grapes
    - Ice cubes
- One-fourth cup of water
- One-inch piece of ginger

Method:

1. Combine carrots, grapes, and orange in a high power blender. Blend until frothy and smooth.
2. Add ice cubes, ginger, and water. Blend the ingredients for thirty seconds.
3. Serve immediately.

Cranberry Smoothie

Total Prep & Cooking Time: One hour and ten minutes

Yields: Two servings

Nutrition Facts: Calories: 155.9| Protein: 2.2g | Carbs: 33.8g | Fat: 1.6g | Fiber: 5.2g

Ingredients

- One cup of almond milk
- Half cup of mixed berries (frozen)
- One-third cup of cranberries
- One banana

Method:

1. Blend mixed berries, banana, and cranberries in a high power food processor. Blend until smooth.
2. Add almond milk and blend again for twenty seconds.
3. Refrigerate the prepared smoothie for one hour.
4. Serve chilled.

Creamsicle Smoothie

Total Prep & Cooking Time: Ten minutes

Yields: Two servings

Nutrition Facts: Calories: 121.3 | Protein: 4.7g | Carbs: 19.8g | Fat: 2.5g | Fiber: 0.3g

Ingredients

- One cup of orange juice
- One and a half cup of crushed ice
- Half cup of milk
- One tsp. of white sugar

Method:

1. Blend milk, orange juice, white sugar, and ice in a high power blender.
2. Keep blending until there is no large chunk of ice. Try to keep the consistency of slushy.
3. Serve immediately.

Sunshine Smoothie

Total Prep & Cooking Time: Thirty minutes

Yields: Four servings

Nutrition Facts: Calories: 176.8 | Protein: 4.2g | Carbs: 39.9g | Fat: 1.3g | Fiber: 3.9g

Ingredients

- Two nectarines (pitted, quartered)
- One banana (cut in chunks)
- One orange (peeled, quartered)
- One cup of vanilla yogurt
- One-third cup of orange juice
- One tbsp. of honey

Method:

1. Add banana chunks, nectarines, and orange in a blender. Blender for two minutes.
2. Add vanilla yogurt, honey, and orange juice. Blend the ingredients until frothy and smooth.
3. Pour the smoothie in glasses and serve.

Chapter 3: Vegetable Smoothies

Apart from fruit smoothies, vegetable smoothies can also provide you with essential nutrients. In fact, vegetable smoothies are tasty as well. So, here are some vegetable smoothie recipes for you.

Mango Kale Berry Smoothie

Total Prep & Cooking Time: Ten minutes

Yields: Four servings

Nutrition Facts: Calories: 117.3 | Protein: 3.1g | Carbs: 22.6g | Fat: 3.6g | Fiber: 6.2g

Ingredients

- One cup of orange juice
- One-third cup of kale
- One and a half cup of mixed berries (frozen)
- Half cup of mango chunks
- One-fourth cup of water
- Two tbsps. of chia seeds

Method:

1. Take a high power blender and add kale, orange juice, berries, mango chunks, chia seeds, and half a cup of water.
2. Blend the ingredients on high settings until smooth.
3. In case the smoothie is very thick, you can adjust the consistency by adding more water.
4. Pour the smoothie in glasses and serve.

Breakfast Pink Smoothie

Total Prep & Cooking Time: Ten minutes

Yields: Two servings

Nutrition Facts: Calories: 198.3 | Protein: 12.3g | Carbs: 6.3g | Fat: 4.5g | Fiber: 8.8g

Ingredients

- One and a half cup of strawberries (frozen)
- One cup of raspberries
- One orange (peeled)

- Two carrots
- Two cups of coconut milk (light)
- One small beet (quartered)

Method:

1. Add strawberries, raspberries, and orange in a blender. Blend until frothy and smooth.
2. Add beet, carrots, and coconut milk.
3. Blend again for one minute.
4. Divide the smoothie in glasses and serve.

Butternut Squash Smoothie

Total Prep & Cooking Time: Five minutes

Yields: Four servings

Nutrition Facts: Calories: 127.3 | Protein: 2.3g | Carbs: 32.1g | Fat: 1.2g | Fiber: 0.6g

Ingredients

- Two cups of almond milk
- One-fourth cup of nut butter (of your choice)
- One cup of water
- One and a half cup of butternut squash (frozen)
- Two ripe bananas
- One tsp. of cinnamon (ground)
- Two tbsps. of hemp protein
- Half cup of strawberries
- One tbsp. of chia seeds
- Half tbsp. of bee pollen

Method:

1. Add butternut squash, bananas, strawberries, and almond milk in a blender. Blend until frothy and smooth.

2. Add water, nut butter, cinnamon, hemp protein, chia seeds, and bee pollen. Blend the ingredients f0r two minutes.

3. Divide the smoothie in glasses and enjoy!

Zucchini and Wild Blueberry Smoothie

Total Prep & Cooking Time: Ten minutes

Yields: Three servings

Nutrition Facts: Calories: 190.2 | Protein: 7.3g | Carbs: 27.6g | Fat: 8.1g | Fiber: 5.7g

Ingredients

- One banana
- One cup of wild blueberries (frozen)
- One-fourth cup of peas (frozen)
- Half cup of zucchini (frozen, chopped)
- One tbsp. of each
  - Hemp hearts
  - Chia seeds
  - Bee pollen
- One-third cup of almond milk
- Two tbsps. of nut butter (of your choice)
- Ten cubes of ice

Method:

1. Add blueberries, banana, peas, and zucchini in a high power blender. Blend the ingredients for two minutes.

2. Add chia seeds, hemp hearts, almond milk, bee pollen, nut butter, and ice. Blend the mixture for making a thick and smooth smoothie.

3. Pour the smoothie in glasses and serve with chopped blueberries from the top.

Cauliflower and Blueberry Smoothie

Total Prep & Cooking Time: Five minutes

Yields: Two servings

Nutrition Facts: Calories: 201.9 | Protein: 7.1g | Carbs: 32.9g | Fat: 10.3g | Fiber: 4.6g

Ingredients

- One Clementine (peeled)
- Three-fourth cup of cauliflower (frozen)
- Half cup of wild blueberries (frozen)
- One cup of Greek yogurt
- One tbsp. of peanut butter
- Bunch of spinach

Method:

1. Add cauliflower, Clementine, and blueberries in a blender. Blend for one minute.
2. Add peanut butter, spinach, and yogurt. Pulse the ingredients for two minutes until smooth.
3. Divide the prepared smoothie in glasses and enjoy!

Immunity Booster Smoothie

Total Prep & Cooking Time: Ten minutes

Yields: Two servings

Nutrition Facts: Calories: 301.9 | Protein: 5.4g | Carbs: 70.7g | Fat: 4.3g | Fiber:

8.9g

Ingredients

For the orange layer:

- One persimmon (quartered)
- One ripe mango (chopped)
- One lime (juiced)
- One tbsp. of nut butter (of your choice)
- Half tsp. of turmeric powder
- One pinch of cayenne pepper
- One cup of coconut milk

For the pink layer:

- One small beet (cubed)
- One cup of berries (frozen)
- One pink grapefruit (quartered)
- One-fourth cup of pomegranate juice
- Half cup of water
- Six leaves of mint
- One tsp. of honey

Method:

1. Add the ingredients for the orange layer in a blender. Blend for making a smooth liquid.
2. Pour the orange liquid evenly in serving glasses.
3. Add the pink layer ingredients in a blender. Blend for making a smooth liquid.
4. Pour the pink liquid slowly over the orange layer.
5. Pour in such a way so that both layers can be differentiated.
6. Serve immediately.

Ginger, Carrot, and Turmeric Smoothie

Total Prep & Cooking Time: Forty minutes

Yields: Two servings

Nutrition Facts: Calories: 140 | Protein: 2.6g | Carbs: 30.2g | Fat: 2.2g | Fiber: 5.6g

Ingredients

For carrot juice:

- Two cups of water
- Two and a half cups of carrots

For smoothie:

- One ripe banana (sliced)
- One cup of pineapple (frozen, cubed)
- Half tbsp. of ginger
- One-fourth tsp. of turmeric (ground)
- Half cup of carrot juice
- One tbsp. of lemon juice
- One-third cup of almond milk

Method:

1. Add water and carrots in a high power blender. Blend on high settings for making smooth juice.
2. Take a dish towel and strain the juice over a bowl. Squeeze the towel for taking out most of the juice.
3. Add the ingredients for the smoothie in a blender and blend until frothy and creamy.
4. Add carrot juice and blend again.
5. Pour the smoothie in glasses and serve.

Romaine Mango Smoothie

Total Prep & Cooking Time: Five minutes

Yields: Two servings

Nutrition Facts: Calories: 117.3 | Protein: 2.6g | Carbs: 30.2g | Fat: 0.9g | Fiber: 4.2g

Ingredients

- Sixteen ounces of coconut water
- Two mangoes (pitted)
- One head of romaine (chopped)
- One banana
- One orange (peeled)
- Two cups of ice

Method:

1. Add mango, romaine, orange, and banana in a high power blender. Blend the ingredients until frothy and smooth.
2. Add coconut water and ice cubes. Blend for one minute.
3. Pour the prepared smoothie in glasses and serve.

Fig Zucchini Smoothie

Total Prep & Cooking Time: Ten minutes

Yields: Two servings

Nutrition Facts: Calories: 243.3 | Protein: 14.4g | Carbs: 74.3g | Fat: 27.6g | Fiber: 9.3g

Ingredients

- Half cup of cashew nuts
- One tsp. of cinnamon (ground)
- Two figs (halved)
- One banana
- Half tsp. of ginger (minced)
- One-third tsp. of honey
- One-fourth cup of ice cubes
- One pinch of salt
- Two tsps. of vanilla extract
- Three-fourth cup of water
- One cup of zucchini (chopped)

Method:

1. Add all the listed ingredients in a high power blender. Blend for two minutes until creamy and smooth.
2. Pour the smoothie in serving glasses and serve.

Carrot Peach Smoothie

Total Prep & Cooking Time: Ten minutes

Yields: Two servings

Nutrition Facts: Calories: 191.2 | Protein: 11.2g | Carbs: 34.6g | Fat: 2.7g | Fiber: 5.4g

Ingredients

- Two cups of peach
- One cup of baby carrots
- One banana (frozen)
- Two tbsps. of Greek yogurt
- One and a half cup of coconut water
- One tbsp. of honey

Method:

1. Add peach, baby carrots, and banana in a high power blender. Blend on high settings for one minute.
2. Add Greek yogurt, honey, and coconut water. Give the mixture a whizz.
3. Pour the smoothie in glasses and serve.

Sweet Potato and Mango Smoothie

Total Prep & Cooking Time: Ten minutes

Yields: Two servings

Nutrition Facts: Calories: 133.3 | Protein: 3.6g | Carbs: 28.6g | Fat: 1.3g | Fiber: 6.2g

Ingredients

- One small sweet potato (cooked, smashed)
- Half cup of mango chunks (frozen)
- Two cups of coconut milk
- One tbsp. of chia seeds
- Two tsps. of maple syrup
- A handful of ice cubes

Method:

1. Add mango chunks and sweet potato in a high power blender. Blend until frothy and smooth.
2. Add chia seeds, coconut milk, ice cubes, and maple syrup. Blend again for one minute.
3. Divide the smoothie in glasses and serve.

Carrot Cake Smoothie

Total Prep & Cooking Time: Ten minutes

Yields: Two servings

Nutrition Facts: Calories: 289.3 | Protein: 3.6g | Carbs: 47.8g | Fat: 1.3g | Fiber: 0.6g

Ingredients

- One cup of carrots (chopped)
- One banana
- Half cup of almond milk
- One cup of Greek yogurt
- One tbsp. of maple syrup
- One tsp. of cinnamon (ground)
- One-fourth tsp. of nutmeg
- Half tsp. of ginger (ground)
- A handful of ice cubes

Method

1. Add banana, carrots, and almond milk in a blender. Blend until frothy and smooth.
2. Add yogurt, cinnamon, maple syrup, ginger, nutmeg, and ice cubes. Blend again for two minutes.
3. Divide the smoothie in serving glasses and serve.

Notes:

- You can add more ice cubes and turn the smoothie into slushy.
- You can store the leftover smoothie in the freezer for two days.

Chapter 4: Green Smoothies

Green smoothies can help in the process of detoxification as well as weight loss. Here are some easy-to-make green smoothie recipes for you.

Kale Avocado Smoothie

Total Prep & Cooking Time: Ten minutes

Yields: Two servings

Nutrition Facts: Calories: 401 | Protein: 11.2g | Carbs: 64.6g | Fat: 17.3g | Fiber: 10.2g

Ingredients

- One banana (cut in chunks)
- Half cup of blueberry yogurt
- One cup of kale (chopped)
- Half ripe avocado
- One-third cup of almond milk

Method:

1. Add blueberry, banana, avocado, and kale in a blender. Blend for making a smooth mixture.
2. Add the almond milk and blend again.
3. Divide the smoothie in glasses and serve.

Celery Pineapple Smoothie

Total Prep & Cooking Time: Ten minutes

Yields: Two servings

Nutrition Facts: Calories: 112 | Protein: 2.3g | Carbs: 3.6g | Fat: 1.2g | Fiber: 3.9g

Ingredients

- Three celery stalks (chopped)
- One cup of cubed pineapple
- One banana
- One pear
- Half cup of almond milk
- One tsp. of honey

Method:

1. Add celery stalks, pear, banana, and cubes of pineapple in a food processor. Blend until frothy and smooth.
2. Add honey and almond milk. Blend for two minutes.
3. Pour the smoothie in serving glasses and enjoy!

Cucumber Mango and Lime Smoothie

Total Prep & Cooking Time: Ten minutes

Yields: Two servings

Nutrition Facts: Calories: 165 | Protein: 2.2g | Carbs: 32.5g | Fat: 4.2g | Fiber: 3.7g

Ingredients

- One cup of ripe mango (frozen, cubed)
- Six cubes of ice
- Half cup of baby spinach leaves
- Two leaves of mint
- Two tsps. of lime juice
- Half cucumber (chopped)
- Three-fourth cup of coconut milk
- One-eighth tsp. of cayenne pepper

Method:

1. Add mango cubes, spinach leaves, and cucumber in a high power blender. Blend until frothy and smooth.
2. Add mint leaves, lime juice, coconut milk, cayenne pepper, and ice cubes. Process the ingredients until smooth.
3. Pour the smoothie in glasses and serve.

Kale, Melon, and Broccoli Smoothie

Total Prep & Cooking Time: Ten minutes

Yields: One serving

Nutrition Facts: Calories: 96.3 | Protein: 2.3g | Carbs: 24.3g | Fat: 1.2g | Fiber: 2.6g

Ingredients

- Eight ounces of honeydew melon
- One handful of kale
- Two ounces of broccoli florets
- One cup of coconut water
- Two sprigs of mint
- Two dates
- Half cup of lime juice
- Eight cubes of ice

Method:

1. Add kale, melon, and broccoli in a food processor. Whizz the ingredients for blending.

2. Add mint leaves and coconut water. Blend again.

3. Add lime juice, dates, and ice cubes. Blend the ingredients until smooth and creamy.

4. Pour the smoothie in a smoothie glass. Enjoy!

Kiwi Spinach Smoothie

Total Prep & Cooking Time: Ten minutes

Yields: Two servings

Nutrition Facts: Calories: 102 | Protein: 3.6g | Carbs: 21.3g | Fat: 2.2g | Fiber: 3.1g

Ingredients

- One kiwi (cut in chunks)
- One banana (cut in chunks)
- One cup of spinach leaves
- Three-fourth cup of almond milk
- One tbsp. of chia seeds
- Four cubes of ice

Method:

1. Add banana, kiwi, and spinach leaves in a blender. Blend the ingredients until smooth.
2. Add chia seeds, ice cubes, and almond milk. Blend again for one minute.
3. Pour the smoothie in serving glasses and serve.

Avocado Smoothie

Total Prep & Cooking Time: Ten minutes

Yields: Two servings

Nutrition Facts: Calories: 345 | Protein: 9.1g | Carbs: 47.8g | Fat: 16.9g | Fiber: 6.7g

Ingredients

- One ripe avocado (halved, pitted)
- One cup of milk
- Half cup of vanilla yogurt
- Eight cubes of ice
- Three tbsps. of honey

Method:

1. Add avocado, vanilla yogurt, and milk in a blender. Blend the ingredients until frothy and smooth.
2. Add honey and ice cubes. Blend the ingredients for making a smooth mixture.
3. Serve immediately.

PART IV

Chapter 1: The Fundamentals of a Low Sugar Diet for Diabetics

For people with diabetes, eating can be quite a challenge. After all, it's not easy dealing with the various recommendations made by doctors. The fact is that the following recommended guidelines are essential to keeping your diabetes in check.

You see, it's important to ensure that your blood sugar levels remain in check. One of the easiest and most effective ways to do this is by keeping your sugar and carb intake as low as possible. So, let's take a look at how this occurs when you go on the low-sugar and low-carb, diabetic diet.

Firstly, when you consume carbs and sugars, these are converted into glucose in the bloodstream as the liver metabolizes them. Since carbs are used as a source of energy, the body needs to secrete insulin from the pancreas in order to break down glucose and send it into the cells as functional energy. Then, the body mixes oxygen to create ATP. This is the source of energy that helps you power your body's entire system.

All is good until there is an excess of glucose in the body. When this occurs, the body stores excess glucose as fat. However, there comes a point where the body just can't keep up. This is where insulin resistance happens. In a nutshell, your cells simply stop accepting any more glucose as there is simply too much glucose in the bloodstream.

These are the spikes in blood sugar levels.

This is where the low-carb, low-sugar diet makes a huge difference in your overall health management plan. The rationale is that when you restrict the number of carbs and sugar that you consume, you are basically giving your body the chance to process what's already in the bloodstream and in storage. So, you are creating a deficit that forces the body to use up what it's already stored.

This is how you can get your blood sugar levels in check.

In a manner of speaking, what you are doing is giving your body a break. Therefore, the body has a chance to catch up. When your body eventually catches up, you end up reducing your overall blood sugar levels. In addition, medication is much more effective as there are fewer carbs and glucose to process.

At first, it can be a bit of a psychological shock to think that you have to go on a low-carb, low-sugar diet. In fact, most people think they have to live on lettuce for the rest of their lives. What you will find is that this diet embraces a large number of foods that are very low in carbs and sugar. As a result, you can eat healthy and tasty at the same time.

However, the secret is knowing which foods promote low blood sugar levels. When you discover these foods, you'll find that keeping your diabetes in check doesn't have to be tough. You can still enjoy delicious foods with zero guilt.

Now that's a plan!

Chapter 2: Benefits of a Low Sugar Diet for Diabetics

The low-sugar, low-carb diet is filled with a number of benefits that diabetics can obtain. The best part is that you don't need to wait for an extended period of time to see the benefits. In fact, you can see benefits within a few days of trying out the diet. This is what makes the diet itself so encouraging.

So, here is a list of five benefits you can expect when going on the low-sugar diet.

1. **Reduction in blood sugar levels**

Naturally, this is the most immediate benefit of this diet. As mentioned earlier, when you reduce the amount of carbs and sugar, your body will begin to use up what's already stored in the system. This is why you can begin to see a reduction in your blood sugar levels within a few days. Over time, your blood sugar levels will begin to normalize. So, the diet, along with medication, will prove to be quite effective.

2. Weight loss

Another benefit is weight loss. Since the body converts glucose into fat when it's stored, a reduction in your carb and sugar consumption will force your body to convert stored fat into energy. This is why folks who go on the low-carb diet begin to see weight loss after a few weeks. While this result isn't immediate, it is almost certain that you'll see weight loss, especially if you are overweight.

3. Increased levels of energy

One of the symptoms that accompany diabetes is low levels of energy. This is due to the imbalance that occurs in the metabolism. Since the metabolism cannot keep up with the amount of carbs and sugar in the bloodstream, it does not produce energy as efficiently as it could. As a result, there are lower levels of energy. When you essentially force your body to process stored up fat, your metabolism becomes more efficient in producing energy. The end result is a boost in energy levels. So, don't be surprised if you find at you feel more energetic after a few days.

4. Hormonal regulation

Hormones tend to go out of whack when there are increased levels of blood sugar. For instance, insulin is the first hormone that goes haywire. However, other hormones are affected as well, such as cortisol (it is associated with weight gain) or epinephrine (used to breakdown and release nutrients in the blood). These hormones tend to work inefficiently when there is a high level of blood sugar. As a result, you may not be getting the most nutrition out of the foods you eat.

5. Improved cognitive function

Sugar, in general, works like a fuel in your body. So, when you consume a large amount of sugar, you get the rush that can power you through a given time period. However, sugar is a very poor fuel as your brain burns right through it. The end result is a severe crash afterward. Over time, your brain builds up "gunk." This gunk limits the brain's capabilities. As such, when you replace sugar with other types of fuels, such as vegetable-based carbs, then your brain produces energy more effectively. It's like putting diesel into an unleaded engine. Sure, the car will run, but it will run poorly. This is why many folks on the low-sugar diet report improved cognitive abilities, thereby reducing the phenomenon known as "brain fog."

With these benefits, you can't go wrong with the low-sugar diet!

Chapter 3: Savory Recipe Ideas

Savory Idea #1: Tangy Cabbage Treat

Number of people served: 4

Time you'll need: 33 to 37 minutes

Calories: 253

Fats: 22.8 g

Proteins: 7.9 g

Carbs: 4.7 g

What you'll require:

- Jalapeno Peppers (two, chopped)
- Cabbage (one Head)
- Pepper & salt (as preferred)
- Onion (one, chopped)
- Bacon (six, strips)

What you need to do:

1. Firstly, cook bacon as per the directions on the pack. While you allow the bacon to reach its optimal point, ready cabbage, and onions by chopping into smaller bite-sized morsels.
2. Once the bacon has been prepared to your preference, take it out of the pan and toss the onion and cabbage in. Please ensure to mix up

everything with the leftover grease from the bacon while simmering in low fire.

3. Next, get the jalapenos ready by cutting up into pieces as small as you like. Feel free to throw in with the other elements.
4. After the vegetables have reached their optimal point, take the crispy bacon and crumble over the entire mix. Add pepper & salt, along with any other low-carb or low-sugar spices.
5. Lastly, toss everything around until the entire mix is thoroughly even. Serve and enjoy!

Savory Idea #2: Low-carb Egg &Veggie Bites

Number of people served: 6

Time you'll need: 11 to 14 minutes

Calories: 21.8

Fats: 3.7 g

Proteins: 4.3 g

Carbs: 1.8 g

What you'll require:

- Bell Pepper (75 g, Chopped)
- Cucumber (45 g, Chopped)
- Spinach (225 g, Chopped)
- Tomato (75 g, Chopped)
- Eggs (three)
- Salt (as preferred)

What you need to do:

1. To get started, set up oven to 180 degrees Celsius along with a muffin tray. The smaller trays are better as they allow for smaller portions if you wish.
2. Next, use a mixing container and place eggs (cracked) inside. Whisk briskly until they are thoroughly mixed.
3. Now, coat trays with your choice of grease (for instance, non-stick spray). Please ensure to leave some extra for the vegetables (chopped)
4. Then, place eggs in the spaces in the tray and toss in vegetables are per your preference. Please make sure to stir so that the mix is distributed evenly. Then, place in the heat for roughly 11 to 14 minutes.
5. Lastly, make sure to check the mixture is cooked all the way through. Serve as a breakfast treat or yummy snack.

Savory Idea #3: Yummy Chicken Dee-light

Number of people served: 2

Time you'll need: 35 to 40 minutes

Calories: 794.7

Fats: 39.1 g

Proteins: 44.2 g

Carbs: 3.3 g

What you'll require:

- Rosemary Leaves (10 g)
- Pepper & salt (as preferred)
- Garlic (cloves, six, minced)
- Chicken Breast (455 g boneless & skinless)
- Cheddar Cheese (70 g, shredded)
- Butter (55 g)

What you need to do:

1. Firstly, set up your oven to a temperature of approximately 190 degrees Celsius. While the oven gain temperature, prepare a tray with grease (your choice).
2. Next, add seasoning to chicken to your liking.
3. Then, begin to prepare garlic butter. Take pan or skillet and set to medium fire on the range. Once the butter has thoroughly melted, toss in garlic and let cook for roughly five to six minutes. Once this time has passed, garlic should be brownish, but make sure it is not burnt. Now, cover chicken with this butter & garlic mix.
4. Once this mix is prepared, set into the oven for about ½ an hour. Make sure to check the chicken so that it is fully cooked all the way through to the center. Once this has been achieved, add cheese as a topping. Allow to melt.
5. Serve by adding some more butter & garlic mix on top. Enjoy!

Savory Idea #4: Low-carb Fried Chicken Surprise

Number of people served: 6

Time you'll need: 33 minutes

Calories: 768

Fats: 54.1 g

Proteins: 59.2 g

Carbs: 1.9 g

What you'll require:

- Pork (rinds, 85 g)
- Pepper & salt (as preferred)
- Lard (according to need)
- Egg (one)
- Chicken (thighs, six)

What you need to do:

1. First, heat up iron pan or skillet on a range top. Then, place eggs in a mixing container for whisking.
2. Next, prepare rinds by crumbling. Upon completion, coat chicken pieces with egg (you can use a brush or dip) and season as per your liking with salt & pepper.
3. Now, take covered chicken pieces and roll over in the rind crumbs. Do this for every piece.
4. After, add in about half an inch of lard (or cooking oil) into pan or skillet. Wait until it reaches the boiling point. Then, place chicken pieces into the fire. Leave for about four to six minutes on each side. Please make sure they are cooked all the way through.
5. Please ensure to turn chicken around at least twice to ensure proper cooking. Serve with a side of crispy veggies or veggie chips.

Savory Idea #5: Low-Sugar Beef Explosion

Number of people served: 4

Time you'll need: one hour

Calories: 331

Fats: 26.7 g

Proteins: 18.7 g

Carbs: 2.1 g

What you'll require:

- Garlic (cloves, two, chopped)
- Coconut grounds (55 g)
- Onions (green, three)
- Coconut Oil (45 g)
- Ginger (10 g, grated)
- Steak (Flat-iron, 455 g)

What you need to do:

1. First, get steak ready by cutting it up into long, thin slices. Upon completion, place into a large freezer bag so that you can add ginger, coconut grounds, and garlic. Then, place into refrigeration so it can marinate for about one hour's time.
2. Next, put a pan or skillet to heat. Add oil for the meat. Heat up for about three to four minutes until it is at boiling point. Then, toss in steak and let sit until thoroughly cooked. This should take about five to seven minutes.

3. After, add in onions (green) to give the flavor a kick. Let everything sit for a minute or two until the texture is as per your liking.
4. Lastly, take some of the marinade from the freezer bag and add in right before turning off the fire. This will add an extra kick. Serve over zucchini pasta or low-carb couscous.

Savory Idea #6: Tangy Pork Extravaganza

Number of people served: 4

Time you'll need: 34 to 37 minutes

Calories: 466.1

Fats: 32.3 g

Proteins: 47.2 g

Carbs: 2.7 g

What you'll require:

- Stock (chicken, 55 g)

- Pepper (7.5 g)
- Pork (chops, four)
- Milk (202 g)
- Coriander (9 g)
- Thyme (dried, 14.5 g)
- Garlic (cloves, two, minced)
- Butter (47 g)
- Salt (14.5 g)
- Oregano (dried, 14.5 g)

What you need to do:

1. First, get chops ready by placing them on a baking sheet. Sprinkle with pepper & salt to season. Please ensure that seasoning is evenly distributed to guarantee flavor. Let sit for one hour. Once time has passed, carefully rinse chops of excess fluid.
2. Next, set the pan to high heat on range top. Place garlic & butter to stir. Once the garlic is fully transparent, the time has come to add in chops on top.
3. Once chops are placed, cook them through for roughly four to six minutes on both sides. Then, let simmer for another minute, or so, to enable flavors to combine. Remove and set aside.
4. Then, on low fire, throw in stock (chicken), and some milk. Scrape the little leftover bits from the chops. Upon completion, toss oregano, coriander, and thyme in. Please ensure you are only simmering and not boiling the sauce.
5. Lastly, as the sauce thickens, turn the heat off and toss chops back into skillet. Combine all elements and add more pepper & salt if desired. Serve with veggies or a fresh salad.

Savory Idea #7: Filet & Cheese Supreme

Number of people served: 3 or 4

Time you'll need: 31 to 36 minutes

Calories: 211

Fats: 17.4 g

Proteins: 11.9 g

Carbs: 2.25 g

What you'll require:

- Paprika (4.5 g)
- Fish Fillet (225 g)
- Parsley (flakes, 7.5 g)
- Pepper (black, 4.5 g)
- Oil (Olive, 18.5 g)
- Cheese (Parmesan, 45 g)

What you need to do:

1. First, heat up the oven to approximately 180 degrees Celsius.
2. Now, get mixing container for the pepper (black), paprika, cheese (Parmesan), and parsley.
3. Then, cover filets with the spice mix. Add oil (olive) and then rollup the mixture ensuring an even coating.
4. Once the fish is ready, set the filets on to tray and place it into the oven for roughly fourteen to seventeen minutes.
5. Lastly, double-check fish is thoroughly cooked and place cheese on top to create a crust. Let sit for a few moments, until cheese is crispy, remove, and serve. Enjoy with veggies or low-carb brown rice.

Savory Idea #8: Quick and Easy Low-carb Chips

Number of people served: 4

Time you'll need: 28 to 34 minutes

Calories: 91.7

Fats: 8.1 g

Proteins: 3.2 g

Carbs: 2.8 g

What you'll require:

- Salt (as preferred)
- Pepper (as preferred)
- Bacon (slices, eight)
- Oil (Olive, 18.5 g)

What you need to do:

1. First, set up an oven to approximately 180 degrees Celsius.
2. Next, grease a tray with oil (olive) or your choice of grease. Then, break up the bacon into small, bite-sized pieces.
3. After, season with pepper & salt as per your taste.
4. Then, throw into the oven for roughly eighteen to twenty-one minutes. Remove and let cool.
5. Once cool to touch, take bits and put into a skillet, or pan, over medium fire. This process usually takes about four to six minutes. Remove from fire and serve as chips. You can serve with a low-fat, low-carb dip as an appetizer!

Savory Idea #9: Unbelievably Low-carb South Treat

Number of people served: 3 to 4

Time you'll need: 29 to 32 minutes

Calories: 288

Fats: 22.3 g

Proteins: 18.9 g

Carbs: 2.7 g

What you'll require:

- Turkey Breast (roasted, 225 g, chopped)
- Cheese (Parmesan, 75 g)
- Cheddar Cheese (shredded, 225 g)
- White Cheddar Cheese (shredded, 225 g)

What you need to do:

1. First, set up an oven to approximately 180 degrees Celsius.
2. Next, take a mixing container and combine all cheeses. You can whisk or use an electric mixer. Then, take a spoonful of the mix and place onto baking sheet in a clump. Lay down as you would with cookies. Space clumps about one inch apart.
3. Upon filling sheet, throw into over for roughly seven to eight minutes. Please ensure that chips do not get burned. Chips are cooked thoroughly when edges turn light to a golden brown. Then, remove and let cool all the way.
4. Lastly, chop up turkey breast and serve chips with a low-sugar dip. Serve as a snack or entrée.

Savory Idea #10: Low-sugar Italian Snack Option

Number of people served: 4 to 6

Time you'll need: About 22 minutes

Calories: 226

Fats: 23.7 g

Proteins: 18.4 g

Carbs: 5.7 g

What you'll require:

- Mozzarella Cheese (shredded, 225 g)
- Pepper (as preferred)
- Seasoning (Italian, 14.5 g)
- Pepperoni (115 g, chopped)
- Garlic (powder, 8.5 g)
- Salt (as preferred)
- Additional choice: Marinara Sauce for Dipping

What you need to do:

1. First, set up an oven to approximately 180 degrees Celsius.
2. Next, take a small muffin tray and coat with spray (cooking). Leave to one side.
3. Then, in a mixing container, combine pepper & cheese, garlic (powder), salt, and seasoning (Italian). Mix cheese thoroughly and add in the

seasoning. Place spoonful of mixture into the bottom of each space on tray.

4. After, top each space with pepperoni. Once ready, place into the oven for about eight to ten minutes. After this time, the cheese should be melted all the way through and light brown around the sides.
5. Lastly, remove, let cool, and serve with low-sugar sauce (marinara works best). Serve as a snack or side for a meat dish.

Chapter 4: Gourmet Recipe Ideas

Gourmet Idea #1: Tasty Chicken and Veggie Pot

Number of people served: 4 to 6
Time you'll need: 26 to 32 minutes

Calories: 238
Fats: 10.9g
Proteins: 27.6g
Carbs: 2.7g

What you'll require:

- Broccoli (one bag, frozen)
- Chicken (115g, shredded)
- Garlic Powder (as preferred)
- Soup (Cream of Mushroom, one can)
- Pepper (as preferred)
- Cheese (Cheddar 221g)

What you need to do:

1. First, prepare the oven to approximately 185 degrees Celsius.
2. Then, in a mixing container, toss in the various elements you will be using (chicken, cheese, and spices)
3. Next, add in soup.
4. Then, place the mixture into a baking container and insert it into the oven.
5. After, let cook in the oven for about twenty-five to thirty minutes.
6. Lastly, ensure that the soup has been thoroughly cooked and cheese properly melted. Serve with a side of crispy veggies or almond breadsticks.

Gourmet Idea #2: Delicious Low-sugar Chicken Meal

Number of people served: 4

Time you'll need: Approximately 30 minutes

Calories: 384

Fats: 21.1g

Proteins: 48.1g

Carbs: 3.2g

What you'll require:

- Cream (Sour, 221 g)
- Salt (9.5 g)
- Chicken (Breast, 1kg, no bone)
- Garlic (Powder, 14.5g)
- Pepper (4.5 g)
- Cheese (Parmesan, 165g, grated)

What you need to do:

1. First, prepare the oven to approximately 185 degrees Celsius.
2. Next, prepare a baking container with grease (or your choice such as spray)
3. After, in a mixing tray, add sour cream and a cup of cheese (Parmesan)
4. Then, place the chicken (breast) into the tray while spreading the mix atop each piece. Also, cover lightly with leftover cheese.
5. After that, insert the tray into the oven. Let it sit there for about twenty-seven to twenty-nine minutes.
6. Lastly, remove once thoroughly cooked and serve with your favorite low-carb side.

Gourmet Idea #3: Italian Chicken Dinner Delight

Number of people served: 2 to 4

Time you'll need: Approximately 25 minutes

Calories: 581

Fats: 41.1g

Proteins: 48.2g

Carbs: 6.1g

What you'll require:

- Garlic (Cloves, two, Minced)
- Tomatoes (Sun-dried, 65g)
- Spinach (221g, Chopped)
- Chicken (Breast, four)
- Paprika (8.5g)
- Cream (Heavy, 221 g)
- Garlic (Powder, 8.5g)
- Butter (14.5 g)
- Salt (8.5g)

What you need to do:

1. First, combine garlic (powder), paprika, and salt into mixing container. Upon completion, use this mixture to coat chicken lightly.
2. Next, fire up a skillet, or pan, and throw in two spoonfuls of butter at the base. Let the butter melt. After this, add in properly seasoned

chicken and let cook thoroughly. This would take about five minutes per side. Please ensure chicken is cooked all the way through. Remove and place to one side.

3. Then, add in the rest of the elements: tomatoes, cream, and tomatoes. It will take about three minutes on low fire for the mix to thicken. After, toss in spinach and mix up everything for four more minutes.
4. Lastly, throw the chicken back into the mix so that all flavors can combine. Ensure that chicken is properly cooked and season further if needed. Serve with a side of veggies, zucchini pasta, or low-carb couscous.

Gourmet Idea #4: Yummy Lemon Beef Surprise

Number of people served: 4
Time you'll need: Approximately three hours

Calories: 507
Fats: 35.1g
Proteins: 44.8g
Carbs: 3.1g

What you'll require:

- Pepper (4.5g)
- Lemon (one)
- Garlic (Cloves, four, Crushed)
- Salt (4.5 g)
- Beef (one kg, Cubed)
- Parsley (26g, Minced)

What you need to do:

1. First, prepare the oven to approximately 167 degrees Celsius.
2. Then, prepare a baking container with foil lining.
3. Next, get a mixing container and cover beef (cubed) with juice (lemon), some zest (lemon), salt, and garlic as preferred. Once it is ready to taste, fold over foil to create a small package.
4. Then, when the package is ready, insert into the middle section of the oven and let sit for roughly three hours. This longer cooking time is intended to let the meat soften to its best point.
5. Lastly, remove the package and let sit for about five or six minutes. Cover meat with more juice (lemon) and sprinkle parsley on top. Serve with your favorite low-carb side.

Gourmet Idea #5: Gourmet Sirloin Option

Number of people served: 3 to 4

Time you'll need: 25 to 30 minutes

Calories: 389

Fats: 18.9g

Proteins: 47.1g

Carbs: 2.3g

What you'll require:

- Garlic (Cloves, four, Crushed)
- Oil (Olive, 12g)
- Pepper & salt (as preferred)
- Steak (Sirloin, 945g, Cubed)
- Butter (14.5 g)

What you need to do:

1. First, get an iron skillet or pan and place it on high heat and place oil (olive).
2. Next, add in pepper & salt to the steak as per your preference.
3. Once the steak has been seasoned according to your preference, place it in the hot skillet, or pan, with hot oil. Let the steak in the hot oil for about four minutes on each side. Turnover twice. Then remove. After, using the same skillet, or pan, toss in butter and garlic. Please ensure to move constantly, so the mix doesn't get burnt.

4. When the garlic is light or golden brown. Place meat for another couple of minutes on each side. Let simmer until the flavors are combined. Serve with your favorite side.

Gourmet Idea #6: Unbelievably Low-sugar Surprise

Number of people served: 4 to 6

Time you'll need: Approximately 20 minutes

Calories: 171

Fats: 11.8g

Proteins: 14.6g

Carbs: 2.9g

What you'll require:

- Cheese (Mozzarella, 100g, Shredded)
- Cheese (Parmesan, 75g, Grated)
- Cheddar Cheese (Shredded, 75g)
- Eggs (two)
- Ham (221g, Diced)

What you need to do:

1. First, set up oven to 185 degrees Celsius.
2. Next, get a mixing container so you can combine egg and the various types of cheeses (shredded). After thoroughly mixing, toss in ham (diced) and continue combining until mixture is evenly distributed.
3. After, get a baking container so it can be greased (your choice of grease).
4. Now, separate mixture into eight round balls or rolls.
5. Then, insert the baking container into the oven for approximately twenty minutes. The rolls will be ready once the cheese has melted, and a golden-brown crust has formed.
6. Lastly, remove the dish and allow it to cool. Serve with chicken or any other meat of your choice.

Gourmet Idea #7: Low-carb Salmon Delight

Number of people served: 3 to 4

Time you'll need: 18 to 24 minutes

Calories: 276

Fats: 19.1g

Proteins: 24.5g

Carbs: 3.7g

What you'll require:

- Rosemary (Fresh, two Springs)
- Lemon (55 g)
- Pepper (as preferred)
- Garlic (Cloves, three)
- Salt (4.5 g)
- Salmon (Filets, four)
- Butter (Unsalted, 8.5g)

What you need to do:

1. First, start out by setting the oven to 202 degrees Celsius.
2. Next, line baking container with a sheet of paper (parchment) and set to the side.
3. Then, rinse out filets (salmon) and pat down to try. Upon completion, place on the baking container with the skin facing down.
4. After, take some soft butter to cover the top of the filer. Also, add in some pepper & salt according to your liking.
5. Now, add the spices (rosemary) and the garlic. Cover the filet and insert it into the oven for roughly thirteen to sixteen minutes.
6. Lastly, remove the filet when thoroughly cooked. Add some juice (lemon) to add a tangy zest. Serve with a side of veggies for a nutritious meal.

Gourmet Idea #8: Shrimp-Avocado Treat

Number of people served: 4

Time you'll need: 30 to 35 minutes

Calories: 539

Fats: 45.2g

Proteins: 25.8g

Carbs: 6.1g

What you'll require:

- Onion (62.5g)
- Cooked shrimp (455g, Chopped)
- Eggs (two)
- Seasoning (Seafood, 4.5g)
- Juice (Lemon, 8.5g)
- Parsley (Fresh, 14.5g)
- Crab (Cooked 125g)
- Avocados (four)
- Cheese (Cheddar, 221 g, Shredded)

What you need to do:

1. First, start out by setting the oven to 177 degrees Celsius.
2. Then, in a mixing container, combine the ingredients: eggs, seasoning (seafood), juice (lemon), onion (chopped), cheese (cheddar), parsley, shrimp, and crab.
3. Next, as the stuffing is completed, cut up avocados in half and remove the pit. Then replace the pit with the stuffing.
4. Lastly, insert the avocados in the oven for roughly twenty-seven minutes. Remove from oven and serve with almond breadsticks.

Gourmet Idea #9: Gourmet Hot Pot Surprise

Number of people served: 4 to 6
Time you'll need: Approximately 45 minutes

Calories: 287
Fats: 20.8g
Proteins: 21.9g
Carbs: 4.8g

What you'll require:

- Cheese (Swiss, 70g, Shredded)
- Pepper (as preferred)
- Garlic (Cloves, four, Minced)
- Fish (Filet, your choice, 455g)
- Shrimp (455g)
- Cream (Heavy, 87g)
- Paprika (as preferred)
- Salt (as preferred)

What you need to do:

1. First, start out by setting the oven to 191 degrees Celsius.
2. Next, prepare a baking container with grease (your choice).
3. Then, cut the filet (fish) into small to medium-sized pieces and place them on the bottom of the baking container. Then, place a layer of shrimp on top of the fish. Add pepper & salt as per your liking.
4. After, when you have everything layered, add in garlic and heavy cream to cover. Upon liberally covering, add cheese (Swiss) on top. Add a touch of paprika for that tangy edge.
5. Now, insert into the oven for roughly sixteen to eighteen minutes. Check often to make sure it does not overcook.
6. Lastly, serve with almond bread!

Gourmet Idea #10: Low-carb Tuna Wraps Treat

Number of people served: 4

Time you'll need: About 10 minutes

Calories: 109

Fats: 5.7g

Proteins: 7.8g

Carbs: 7.1g

What you'll require:

- Yogurt (Greek, 50g)
- Wrap (Wheat, four)
- Bell Pepper (Red, 25g, Diced)
- Spinach (45g)
- Celery (65g, Diced)
- Tuna (one can)

What you need to do:

1. First, drain liquid from the can, and place tuna into a mixing container. Once this is in place, add in the red bell pepper, celery, and the Greek yogurt. Combine elements together well, so the vegetables and tuna are combined thoroughly.
2. Next, you are going to want to place the mixture into the middle of the whole-wheat wraps and top off with the spinach.
3. Serve with veggie chips and lemonade for a refreshing brunch treat.

Chapter 5: Quick and Easy Recipe Ideas

Quick and Easy Idea #1: Quick and Easy Veggie Treat

Number of people served: 4

Time you'll need: 35 to 40 minutes

Calories: 51

Fats: 3.1 g

Proteins: 4.5 g

Carbs: 2.3 g

What you'll require:

- Egg (whites, two)
- Spinach (221g, chopped)
- Eggs (whole, two)
- Pepper (Bell, one)
- Salsa (14.5g)
- Onion (35g, chopped)
- Pepper & salt (as preferred)

What you need to do:

1. First, place the pan over medium fire. Once it is warm, throw in some oil (olive) and start by placing spinach and onion until reaching consistency to your preference. Season with pepper plus salt. Add more salsa if you wish.

2. Next, let your vegetables cook, cut up a bell pepper in two slices to create a small bowl. Upon completion, add the spinach mix to the pepper bowls and the open an egg on top.

3. Then, insert into the oven for about 25 to 28 minutes. Make sure to see that egg is thoroughly prepared.

4. Lastly, serve as a side to your favorite meat dish.

Quick and Easy Idea #2: Spicy Egg and Veggie Dash

Number of people served: 12

Time you'll need: 30 to 35 minutes

Calories: 242

Fats: 21.7 g

Proteins: 10.2 g

Carbs: 1.1 g

What you'll require:

- Bacon (in strips, 11)
- Onion (Powder, 4.5g)
- Garlic (Powder, 4.5g)
- Cheese (cream, 95g)
- Pepper & salt (as preferred)
- Eggs (8)
- Peppers (Jalapeno, four, Chopped)
- Cheese (Cheddar, 121 g)

What you need to do:

1. First, fire up the oven to 165 degrees Celsius.
2. Then, fire up bacon until crispy.
3. Next, in another container, mix up chopped jalapenos, eggs, cheese (cream), and seasoning. Toss in leftover bacon grease.

4. Then, take a muffin baking container and fill the edge of each space with bacon. Upon completion, pour in the mix down the middle of each space. Fill up to about 2/3 of the way. This is important as eggs will rise.
5. After, add some cheese (cheddar) and some jalapeno to provide spice. Insert into the oven and let cook for about 22 to 24 minutes. These will be ready when eggs are thoroughly done and fluffy.
6. Lastly, remove and serve as a snack or an appetizer.

Quick and Easy Idea #3: Low-sugar Hot Cake Surprise

Number of people served: 10

Time you'll need: Approximately 20 minutes

Calories: 133

Fats: 11.8 g

Proteins: 5.3 g

Carbs: 1.9 g

What you'll require:

- Flour (Almond, 221 g)

- Eggs (4)
- Milk (Almond, Non-sugar, 36.5g)
- Extract (Vanilla, 7.5g)
- Baking Powder (4.7g)
- Oil (Olive, 18.5g)

What you need to do:

1. First, in a mixing container, mix up baking powder, extract (vanilla), milk (almond), flour (almond), and eggs. Please ensure all clumps are removed.
2. Next, use a tablespoon to place mixture into pan or skillet. Prepare these as you would regular pancakes.
3. Last, top with butter or non-sugar syrup.

Quick and Easy Idea #4: Cheesy Veggie Bites

Number of people served: 4

Time you'll need: Approximately 30 minutes

Calories: 161

Fats: 11.6 g

Proteins: 11.4 g

Carbs: 5.1 g

What you'll require:

- Flour (Almond, 36.5g)
- Onion (36.5g, minced)

- Seasoning (Mexican, 8.5g)
- Mozzarella (221g, shredded)
- Broccoli (225g)
- Salt (as preferred)
- Garlic (clove, one, minced)
- Cilantro (17.5g)
- Egg (one)
- Pepper (as preferred)

What you need to do:

1. First, set up 201 degrees Celsius.
2. Next, prepare a baking container by lining with parchment paper.
3. Then, steam broccoli in a pot (5 minutes) or microwave (1-2 minutes). Tenderize broccoli to make chopping easier.
4. After, cut up broccoli into small chunks. Throw everything into mixing container (parsley, cheese, flour, egg, and spices). Mix up thoroughly until evenly distributed.
5. Now, roll up into a small ball and distribute evenly throughout the baking container.
6. Once completed, cover with some oil (olive) and insert it into the oven for about 26 to 28 minutes.
7. Lastly, serve with low-carb dip as a snack.

Quick and Easy Idea #5: Low-carb Pudding Dee-light

Number of people served: 4

Time you'll need: 18 to 20 minutes

Calories: 132

Fats: 12.1g

Proteins: 13.8g

Carbs: 1.4g

What you'll require:

- Coconut (125g, shredded)
- Almonds (221g, chopped)
- Chia seed (221g)
- Milk (almond, 225g)

What you need to do:

1. First, measure out all of the fixings and add to the Instant Pot, stirring well.
2. Then, secure the lid and select the high setting (2-5 minutes)
3. Lastly, quick release the pressure and place the pudding into four serving glasses.

Quick and Easy Idea #6: Tangy Egg Salad

Number of people served: 4 to 5

Time you'll need: 26 to 32 minutes

Calories: 314

Fats: 25.7g

Proteins: 15.4g

Carbs: 1.4g

What you'll require:

- Bacon (strips, five, raw)
- Paprika (smoked, 14.5)
- Eggs (large, 10)
- Onion (green, 36.5g)
- Mayonnaise (125g)
- Mustard (Dijon, 45g)
- Pepper & salt (as preferred)

Also required: 6-7-inch baking container

What you need to do:

1. First, grease up all sides of the pan inside of pot on the trivet. Toss one cup of cold water in the bottom of the Instant Pot and add the steam rack.
2. Next, open up eggs in a pan.
3. Then, insert pan on rack. Secure the lid and set the timer for 6 minutes (high-pressure). Natural release the pressure to remove pan.
4. After, remove any moisture. Flip pan over on a wooden cutting board for egg loaf to release. Cut up and place it into a mixing dish.
5. Now, clean the Instant Pot container and choose the sauté function (medium fire). Prepare bacon till crispy.
6. After that, add in chopped eggs with mustard, mayo, paprika, pepper, and salt. Top with green onion.
7. Lastly, serve as a side with your favorite meat dish.

Quick and Easy Idea #7: Cheesy Egg Cups

Number of people served: 4

Time you'll need: 12 to 16 minutes

Calories: 117

Fats: 8.8g

Proteins: 8.7g

Carbs: 1.8g

What you'll require:

- Eggs (four)
- Cheese (Cheddar, 125g, shredded)
- Veggies (diced, your choice, veggies tomatoes, mushrooms, and/or peppers, 221g)
- Milk (low-fat, non-sugar, 221g)
- Pepper & salt (as preferred)
- Cilantro (chopped, 125g)

What you'll require for the Topping:

- Cheese (shredded, your choice, 221g)

Also Required:

1. Jars (medium, four)
2. Water (0.5L)

What you need to do:

1. First, whisk up cheese, veggies, pepper, eggs, milk (low-fat), salt, and cilantro.

1. Next, combine the mix into each jar. Tighten lids (not too tight) to keep water from entering the egg mix.
2. Then, arrange the trivet in the Instant Pot and add the water. Arrange the jars on the trivet and set the timer for 5 minutes (high pressure). When done, quick release the pressure, and top with the rest of the cheese (½ cup).
3. Lastly, broil if you like for 2 to 4 minutes till the cheese is browned to your preference.

Quick and Easy Idea #8: Asparagus Appetizer/Side Salad

Number of people served: 4 to 6

Time you'll need: 18 to 22 minutes

Calories: 221

Fats: 8.6g

Proteins: 15.7g

Carbs: 8.1g

What you'll require:

- Red potatoes (small, 455g)
- Asparagus (fresh, trimmed and chopped lengthwise)
- Tuna (2 tins)
- Olives (Greek, 125g, pit removed)
- Dressing (Italian, low sugar, 45g)

What you need to do:

1. First, chop potatoes and let soak in water for about 5 minutes to let starch drain.
2. Next, put water in the pot, about 2 inches, and heat up to a boiling point. Throw in chopped potatoes to cook for about 12 to 14 minutes.
3. Then, in the remaining 2 to 4 minutes of cooking potatoes, add asparagus to the water.
4. After, turn off the heat, remove water from asparagus and potatoes and then place it into ice water.
5. Lastly, serve with tuna and olives as an appetizer or side for a chicken or fish dish.

Quick and Easy Idea #9: Low-carb Pork Treat

Number of people served: 4 to 6
Time you'll need: 18 to 22 minutes

Calories: 221
Fats: 8.6g
Proteins: 15.7g
Carbs: 8.1g

What you'll require:

- Pork (tenderloin, 455g)
- Salt (14.5g)
- Pepper (18.5g)
- Oil (Olive, 75g)
- Cider (apple, 95g)
- Syrup (maple, non-sugar, 25g)
- Vinegar (apple cider)

What you need to do:

1. First, set up your oven to 190 degrees Celsius.
2. Next, cut up tenderloin into two pieces or to fit in the pan or skillet you are using. Transfer into another container.
3. Then, put oil in pan, or skillet, and then fire up for about 6 to 8 minutes. Toss in vinegar, syrup, and cider while adding pepper until boiling point. Make sure to remove bits stuck to the bottom.
4. After, throw in meat. Prepare thoroughly until the mixture is reduced to glazed texture.
5. Lastly, remove and serve while adding sauce for glazing. Serve with a side of veggies.

Quick and Easy Idea #10: Easy Fish Delight

Number of people served: 4 to 6 Time you'll need: 18 to 22 minutes

Calories: 257

Fats: 8.8g

Proteins: 25.7g

Carbs: 9.2g

What you'll require:

- Breadcrumbs (low-carb, 56g)
- Oil (Olive, 45g)
- Dill (fresh, 45g, snipped)
- Salt (10.5g)
- Pepper (5g)
- Filet (tilapia or salmon, 50g per filet)
- Juice (lemon, 25g)
- Lemon (wedges)

What you need to do:

1. First, set up the oven to 186 degrees Celsius. Add the pepper, oil (olive), dill (fresh), salt, and juice (lemon).
2. Next, add filet (fish of your choice) into a baking container which has been previously coated with grease. Add breadcrumbs on top of fish patting down to so they stick. Coat both sides.
3. Then, let sit in the oven until fish is tender, roughly for 12 to 14 minutes.
4. Lastly, serve with veggies and add lemon wedges on top.

Chapter 6: Low-Carb Recipe Ideas

Low-Carb Recipe Idea #1: Balsamic Roast Delight

Number of people served: 4 to 6

Time you'll need: 35 to 40 minutes

Calories: 51

Fats: 3.1 g

Proteins: 4.5 g

Carbs: 2.3 g

What you'll require:

- Chuck roast (one, no bone, 1.5kg)
- Onion (chopped, 55g)
- Water (0.5L)
- Ground pepper (black, 14.5g)
- Garlic (powder, 14.5g)
- Salt (kosher, 14.5g)
- Vinegar (balsamic, 14.5g)
- Xanthan gum (25g)

For Garnishing:

- Fresh parsley (chopped, 20g)

What you need to do:

1. First, combine the garlic powder, salt, and pepper and spread on the meat to prepare the seasoning.
2. Next, utilize the skillet to sear the meat. Add in the vinegar and deglaze the skillet, or pan, while you let cook for another couple of minutes.
3. Then, toss in onion into a pot along with (two cups) boiling water into the mixture. Cover with a top and allow simmer for thirty to forty minutes on medium-low heat.
4. After, remove meat from pot and add to a cutting surface. Shred up into chunks and throw away any fat and/or bones.
5. Now, add in the xanthan gum to the broth and mix up briskly. Place the thoroughly cooked meat back into the pan to heat up.
6. Lastly, serve with a favorite side dish.

Low-Carb Recipe Idea #2: Burger Calzone Treat

Number of people served: 6
Time you'll need: 25 to 30 minutes

Calories: 400
Fats: 25.1g
Proteins: 24.5 g
Carbs: 2.6 g

What you'll require:

- Mayonnaise (45g)
- Onion (yellow, one diced)
- Beef (ground, 750g, lean)
- Cheese (cheddar, 75g, shredded)
- Flour (Almond, 95g)

- Cheese (Mozzarella, 75g, shredded)
- Egg (one)
- Bacon (4 thin strips)
- Dill pickle (4 spears)
- Cheese (cream, 95g)

What you need to do:

1. First, program the oven to 185 degrees Celsius. Set up a baking container with parchment paper.
2. Next, chop up pickles into lengthy spears. Set to one side when completed.
3. Then, to prepare the crust, combine half of the cream cheese and the mozzarella. Insert into microwave 30 seconds. Upon melting, add egg and almond flour to prepare the dough. Set aside.
4. After, set the beef to fire on the stove using a medium temp setting.
5. Now, cook bacon (microwave for approximately four minutes or on the stovetop with pan or skillet). Upon cooling, break up into bits.
6. Now, dice up an onion and toss into the beef to cook until tenderized. Throw in bacon, pickle bits, cheddar cheese, the rest of the cream cheese, and mayonnaise. Move briskly.
7. After that, roll the dough into a prepared baking container. Place the mixture into the middle of the container. Fold up ends and side to create the calzone.
8. Lastly, insert into until brown or about 12 to 14 minutes. Let it rest for 10 minutes before cutting up.

Low-Carb Recipe Idea #3: Steak Skillet Nacho

Number of people served: 3 to 4

Time you'll need: 26 to 33 minutes

Calories: 376

Fats: 31.5g

Proteins: 19.4g

Carbs: 6.1 g

What you'll require:

- Cheese (Cheddar, 75g)

- Coconut oil (45g)
- Butter (15g)
- Beef (Steak, round tip, 1kg)
- Cauliflower (750g)
- Turmeric (15g)
- Chili (powder, 15g)
- Cheese (Monterey Jack, 75g)

For Garnishing:

- Sour cream (25g)
- Jalapeno (canned, 20g, slices)
- Avocado (105g)

What you need to do:

1. First, set up oven temp to 176 degrees Celsius.
2. Next, prepare the cauliflower into chip-like shapes.
3. After, combine the chili powder, turmeric, and coconut oil in a mixing container.
4. Then, throw in cauliflower and add it to a container. Set the timer for 18 to 24 minutes.
5. Now, over a med-high fire in a cast iron pan, place butter. Fire up until both sides are thoroughly done, flipping only one time. Let it sit for six to nine minutes. Slice up thinly and add in some pepper and salt to the meat.
6. After that, move the florets to the pan and add in the steak bits. Top it off with the cheese and bake six to nine more minutes.
7. Lastly, serve with your favorite side of veggies.

Low-Carb Recipe Idea #4: Portobello Burger Meal

Number of people served: 4

Time you'll need: 22 to 27 minutes

Calories: 327

Fats: 23.1g

Proteins:19.4g

Carbs: 6.1 g

What you'll require:

- Mushroom (Portobello, 6 caps)
- Beef (ground, 455g, lean)
- Pepper (Black, 6g, ground)
- Worcestershire sauce (14.5g)
- Salt (pink or kosher, 12g)
- Cheese (cheddar, 56g or 6 slices)
- Oil (avocado, 12g)

What you need to do:

1. First, remove the stem, rinse, and dab dry the mushrooms.
2. Then, combine the salt, pepper, beef, and Worcestershire sauce in a mixing container. Shape into patties.
3. After, fire up the oil (medium fire). Let caps simmer about four to five minutes on each side.
4. Next, move the mushrooms to a bowl, utilizing the same pan, prepare the patties for six minutes, turn, and prepare another six minutes until ready.
5. Now, combine the cheese to the patties and cover for about a minute to melt the cheese.
6. Lastly, add a mushroom cap to burgers along with the desired garnish to serve.

Low-Carb Recipe Idea #5: Low-carb Super Chili

Number of people served: 4
Time you'll need: 20 to 24 minutes

Calories: 319
Fats: 24.1g
Proteins:39.2g
Carbs: 3.4g

What you'll require for the Chili:

- Stock (beef or chicken, 25g)
- Steak (1kg, cubed into 1-inch cubes)
- Leeks (sliced, 25g)
- Cumin (4g)
- Cayenne pepper (ground, 4g)
- Pepper (black, 4g)
- Salt (4g)
- Whole tomatoes (canned with juices, 221g)
- Chili powder (2.5g)

Additional Toppings:

- Cheese (cheddar, 221g, shredded)
- Sour cream (95g)
- Cilantro (fresh, 25g, chopped)
- Avocado (one half, sliced or cubed)

What you need to do:

1. First, toss all of the fixings into the cooker - except the toppings.
2. Then, use the cooker's high setting for about six hours.
3. Lastly, serve and add the toppings.

Low-Carb Recipe Idea #6: "You won't believe it's low-carb" Chicken Parmesan

Number of people served: 2 to 4

Time you'll need: 34 to 40 minutes

Calories: 586

Fats: 31.4g

Proteins:55.5g

Carbs: 2.7g

What you'll require:

- Rinds (pork, 221g)
- Sauce (Marinara, 45g)
- Chicken (breast, 455g)
- Cheese (parmesan, 56g)
- Garlic (powder, 12g)
- Pepper & salt (as preferred)
- Egg (one)
- Cheese (Mozzarella, 125g, shredded)
- Oregano (12g)

What you need to do:

1. First, set up an oven temp setting of 165 degrees Celsius.
2. Next, utilize a food processor to mash rinds and cheese (parmesan). Add them to a mixing container.

3. After, pound chicken breasts until they are about one-half inch thick. Whisk up egg and dip chicken in for the egg wash. Place the chicken into crumbs.
4. Then, distribute the breasts on a lightly greased baking container evenly. Add in seasonings and insert them into the oven for approximately 23 to 26 minutes.
5. Now, cover with the marinara sauce over each serving. Top with the mozzarella and bake for 12 to 14 minutes.
6. Lastly, serve with a bed of spinach.

Low-Carb Recipe Idea #7: Tangy Coconut Chicken

Number of people served: 4 to 5

Time you'll need: 25 to 28 minutes

Calories: 492

Fats: 39.7g

Proteins:28.9g

Carbs: 2.3g

What you'll require for the Tenders:

- Egg (large, one)
- Onion (powder, 8.5g)
- Curry (powder, 18.5g)
- Pork rinds (Crumbled, 125g)
- Chicken (thighs, 1kg, no bone or skin, about 6 to 8 pieces)
- Coriander (14.5g)
- Coconut (shredded, 95g, unsweetened)
- Garlic (powder, 8.5g)
- Pepper & salt (as preferred)

What you'll require for spicy and sweet mango sauce dip:

- Sour cream (25g)
- Ginger (ground, 14.5g)
- Mango extract (15g)
- Mayonnaise (25g)
- Sugar-free ketchup(25g)
- Cayenne pepper (14g)
- Liquid stevia (7 to 8 drops)
- Garlic (powder, 8.5g)
- Red pepper (flakes, 5g)

What you need to do:

1. First, program oven to 185 degrees Celsius.
2. Then, whisk the eggs and debone the thighs. Slice them into strips (skins on).
3. Next, add the spices, coconut, and pork rinds to a zipper-type bag. Add the chicken, shake, and place on a wire rack. Bake for about 14 minutes. Flip them over and continue baking for another 18 minutes.
4. Lastly, combine the sauce components and stir well. Serve with your favorite side of veggies or salad.

Low-Carb Recipe Idea #8: Slow cook Chicken Casserole

Number of people served: 3 to 4

Time you'll need: 35 to 45 minutes

Calories: 224

Fats: 9.4g

Proteins:30.4g

Carbs: 5.7g

What you'll require:

- Chicken breasts (two in cubes)
- Bay leaf (one)
- Cheese (Mozzarella, 221g, shredded)
- Tomato sauce (256g or one tine)
- Seasoning (Italian, 14.5g)
- Salt (5.5g)
- Pepper (4g)
- Optional: slow cooker (2-quart)

What you need to do:

1. First, remove the bones from the chicken and chop it into cubes. Add them to the slow cooker.
2. Next, pour in the sauce over the chicken and add the spices. Stir and cook on the low setting for thirty to forty minutes.
3. Lastly, serve with the cheese as a topping.

Low-Carb Recipe Idea #9: Low-carb Roll Up Treat

Number of people served: 2 to 4
Time you'll need: 15 to 20 minutes

Calories: 191
Fats: 7.9g
Proteins:15.6g
Carbs: 1.9g

What you'll require:

- Eggs (large, 6)
- Milk (221g)
- Garlic (powder, 14.5g)
- Salt (kosher, 9.5g)
- Pepper (Black, 9.5g, freshly ground)
- Butter (11g)
- Chives (chopped, 5g)
- Bacon (slices, 12)
- Cheese (cheddar, 105g)

What you need to do:

- First, in mixing container, whisk up eggs together along with milk and garlic (powder). Add in salt & pepper as preferred.
- Next, in skillet or pan, melt butter over medium fire. Toss in eggs and scramble for 2 to 4 minutes. Toss in chives.
- Then, on a cutting surface, cut up bacon slices. Place cheddar on the bottom and then toss in a bunch of eggs. Roll up very closely.
- Lastly, place rolls back into pan, or skillet with the seam facing down. Remove once crispy. Serve with whole-grain toast.

Low-Carb Recipe Idea #10: Cauliflower Cheese Surprise

Number of people served: 2 to 4

Time you'll need: 10 to 20 minutes

Calories: 164

Fats: 6.5g

Proteins: 16.3g

Carbs: 2.4g

What you'll require:

- Cauliflower (one Head, about 256g)
- Eggs (two)
- Cheese (parmesan, 75g)
- Oregano (35g)
- Cheese (cheddar, 75g, shredded)

What you need to do:

- First, cut up cauliflower into individual florets. Place them into a food processor until the texture appears similar to rice. You could also grate if you don't have a processor.
- Then, in a mixing container, combine cauliflower, eggs, cheese (parmesan), and the oregano. Mix up until even and add salt & pepper.
- After, fire up a skillet, or pan, over medium fire. Todd mixture into the pan. Pat down to form a patty. Exert pressure using a spatula. Cook for 4 to 6 minutes. Turn over and repeat on the other side.
- Lastly, sprinkle cheese until it is melted. Make "sandwiches" by putting two pieces together. Serve as a snack or side to your favorite meat dish.

Chapter 7: 7-day Sample Low Sugar Diet Plan

In this chapter, we are presenting a 7-day sample plan to give you an idea of how you can put together a winning combination of healthy foods. Please bear in mind that this is only a guide. So, feel free to customize this plan as you get more experience and develop your own style.

Week One			
Day / Meal	**Breakfast**	**Lunch**	**Dinner**
Monday	Fresh fruit bowl topped with granola and honey	Veggie and chicken club sandwich on whole wheat bread	Chicken and veggie casserole
Tuesday	Spicy breakfast burritos	Bean soup with croutons	Grilled salmon and veggies
Wednesday	Scrambled eggs, bacon and a slice of whole-grain toast	Mixed garden salad, fresh veggies, and grilled chicken	Sirloin and veggies surprise
Thursday	Low-sugar cereal with low-fat	Steak and potatoes with a	Chicken fajitas with mashed

	dairy milk	side of crispy veggies	potatoes
Friday	Veggie cheesy bits	Grilled salmon, sautéed veggies with garlic whole wheat toast	Roast beef club sandwich with crispy plantain bits
Saturday	Low-sugar whole grain flapjacks	Spicy chicken fajita burritos	Veggie pizza with small salad
Sunday	Whole grain veggie breakfast wraps	Tangy Mexican bean bowl with guacamole	Chicken noodles and sautéed veggies

www.ingramcontent.com/pod-product-compliance
Lightning Source LLC
LaVergne TN
LVHW010312070526
838199LV00065B/5539
9789814950831